The Common Market:

Friend or Competitor?

THE CHARLES C. MOSKOWITZ LECTURES　　　NUMBER IV

The Common Market:
Friend or Competitor?

Jesse W. Markham *C. E. Fiero*
PROFESSOR OF ECONOMICS   VICE PRESIDENT

PRINCETON UNIVERSITY   THE CHASE MANHATTAN BANK

Howard S. Piquet
SENIOR SPECIALIST IN INTERNATIONAL ECONOMICS

LEGISLATIVE REFERENCE SERVICE

THE LIBRARY OF CONGRESS

THE CHARLES C. MOSKOWITZ LECTURES
SCHOOL OF COMMERCE, ACCOUNTS, AND FINANCE
NEW YORK UNIVERSITY
NEW YORK UNIVERSITY PRESS   1964

© 1964 BY NEW YORK UNIVERSITY
LIBRARY OF CONGRESS CATALOG CARD NUMBER: 64–18617
MANUFACTURED IN THE UNITED STATES OF AMERICA

FOREWORD

THREE DISTINGUISHED AUTHORITIES in the field of international economics have combined to produce this fourth series of Charles C. Moskowitz Lectures, which examines in depth the political and economic history of the Common Market and its implications for the United States.

In the first chapter, entitled "The Political Economy of the European Economic Community," Jesse W. Markham, Professor of Economics at Princeton University, cites the various postwar forces that led to the creation of the European Economic Community, and then moves on to a discussion of the political and economic forces which have shaped and are shaping the Common Market.

In Chapter 2 Charles E. Fiero, Vice President of the Chase Manhattan Bank, discusses "The American Corporation in the Common Market." He evaluates the over-all effect of American subsidiaries in Europe, with particular emphasis on the impact of direct investments on our balance of payments, the impact of the U.S. corporation on the European economy and social environment, and the impact which American investments in Europe have on our corporate philosophy and structure.

Howard S. Piquet, Senior Specialist in International Economics of the Legislative Reference Service, The Library of Congress, concludes the series with a penetrating discussion of "The European Common Market in Economic Perspective."

The School of Commerce, Accounts, and Finance is honored to have sponsored these definitive lectures, which deal with one of the most important and dramtic occurrences of this century.

John H. Prime, DEAN
SCHOOL OF COMMERCE, ACCOUNTS, AND FINANCE
NEW YORK UNIVERSITY   DECEMBER 1963

THE CHARLES C. MOSKOWITZ LECTURES

THE CHARLES C. MOSKOWITZ LECTURES were established through the generosity of a distinguished alumnus of the School of Commerce, Mr. Charles C. Moskowitz of the Class of 1914, who retired after many years as Vice President-Treasurer and a director of Loew's, Inc.

Mr. Moskowitz's aim in establishing the lectures was to contribute to the understanding of the function of business and its related disciplines in society, by providing a public forum for the dissemination of enlightened business theories and practices.

The School of Commerce, Accounts, and Finance, and New York University are deeply grateful to Mr. Moskowitz for his continued interest in, and contribution to, the educational and public-service program of his alma mater.

CONTENTS

FOREWORD   V
    Dean John H. Prime

THE POLITICAL EONOMY OF THE
EUROPEAN ECONOMIC COMMUNITY   1
    Jesse W. Markham

THE AMERICAN CORPORATION
IN THE COMMON MARKET   43
    Charles E. Fiero

THE EUROPEAN COMMON MARKET
IN ECONOMIC PERSPECTIVE   77
    Howard S. Piquet

1.

THE POLITICAL ECONOMY OF THE
EUROPEAN ECONOMIC COMMUNITY

Jesse W. Markham
Professor of Economics
Princeton University

Introduction

The great significance of the European Economic Community lies not so much in how or why it exists, but in that it exists. At the conference on "The Status of European Integration" invoked in Bologna in the late spring of 1956 the participants' prognosis for a significant step toward a united Europe ranged from pessimism to subdued optimism. The grounds for pessimism were plentiful and visible: Only twenty months earlier the tediously designed plan for the Europen Defense Community had ended abruptly in disillusioning failure, as had all previous attempts at European unification since the days of Charlemagne. It was apparent that any European union that did not include both France and Germany would fall far short of the plan envisaged by the neo-Eurocrats of the Continent. Yet the French government appeared much too unstable even seriously to consider, much less enter into, any enduring relationship with the group of countries eventually to become its Continental partners;

and while under Chancellor Adenauer's West German government the immediate postwar tide of resentment and distrust of Germany had receded, it had not yet ebbed to the low-water mark. Moreover, these more immediate reasons for pessimism were superimposed upon the older, continuous background of cultural, linguistic, political, and economic differences among European nations, and indeed the traditional European dedication to nationalism itself.

Of course there were also grounds for optimism, at least subdued optimism. These grounds consisted not so much of the emergence of strong new forces making for European union but rather of the growing awareness on the part of responsible statesmen and their political constituencies of forces that had been evident to such Eurocrats as Jean Monnet, Robert Schuman, and Paul-Henri Spaak for several decades. To much of Europe, and, significantly, this was especially true of the six countries destined to form the European Economic Community, the ravages of two world wars had deprived nationalism of its purpose. Their traditional policy of neutrality in times of European conflict may still have moved Switzerland and Sweden to pursue national independence, even when *political* independence carried with it larger quantities of *economic* independence than they would otherwise have preferred. The United Kingdom's Commonwealth ties provided her with a conflicting substitute for union with Continental Europe, and her emergence from World War II a victorious nation— at least in the traditional meaning of that term—meant that a workable alternative to nationalism in the context of Commonwealth association was not an urgent matter. But to most of Western Continental Europe nationalism had lost much of its historic purpose, a process that was hastened by the confused and conflicting national policies during the Suez and Hungarian crises of late 1956 and the mounting frustrations growing out of the Cold War.

The decline in the popular appeal of nationalism merely lowered somewhat a still formidable barrier to a united Europe; a significant step in the direction of union, however, required acceptance on the part of member countries of both the positive merits and attainability of the proposed union. The terms "merit" and "attainability" are chosen here with great care because, as I shall argue momentarily, they not only define the threshold at which disintegration and isolated nationalism finally gave way to what was to become the European Economic Community but they are also the crucial determinants of the Community's structure, policies, and membership.

An internationally famous historian, on being asked what the discipline of history included, is reported to have responded, "Why, it is all that has occurred in the past, that which is occurring in the present, and all that will occur in the future." Professional modesty prevents my staking out such infinite bounds for the discipline of economics, but a strong case can now be made that any substantial union of European nations must, in its initial stages, have been essentially economic in character. This does not mean, as the architects and administrators of the European Economic Community have repeatedly pointed out, that in matters relating to the union of Western European nations politics and economics can be separated;[1] indeed, their inseparability accounts for the disinterment of the term "political economy" for inclusion in the title of this essay. But I believe that the received interpretation of the European Economic Community, namely, that economic union is a step consciously taken in the direction of ultimate political union is not an entirely correct assessment of how the economic and political forces have operated to create the Community. Economic integration is neither logically nor in point of historical fact a precedent to political union; in the broad sweep of history, the reverse has been true.

In the course of what is now approaching a period of two hundred years, from Professor Adam Smith to our contemporary the eminent Professor Jacob Viner, the economists' theories supporting the case for free trade and competitive resource allocation, or a "one world" in economic affairs, have been transformed into economic axioms. If we therefore assume that man is sufficiently rational to see the obvious, the irrefutable case for an integrated world-wide economic community would long ago have led us much closer to such a community than we now are. But this economic force, to cast the problem in contemporary economic terms, operates under a strong constraint, the political constraint of nationalism. The European Economic Community has come about because, in the six member countries, this constraint became sufficiently weak to let the forces making for integration

[1] cf. Walter Hallstein, *United Europe: Challenge and Opportunity* (Cambridge, Mass.: Harvard University Press, 1962).

become operative. The Rome Treaty, which created the EEC, gives recognition to both the economic forces making for the geographical mobility of goods, services, and factors of production and the constraint consisting of the reluctance of member countries to relinquish control over their domestic and international affairs. It is now in fact and in title the European Economic Community. It is only hopefully the first significant step toward a fully integrated European Community.

Absent this interpretation, the present EEC is a highly improbable assortment of nations from which to form a political and economic union. The six member countries represent four different languages. The German tradition has been to sacrifice considerable individual liberty for the sake of organized order and national purpose. The tradition of France has been to sacrifice national purpose and organized order, sometimes even order, for the preservation of individual liberty. There are significant structural differences in the larger national economies. In 1958 central government expenditures accounted for 25 percent [2] of France's gross national product; it is estimated that nationalized enterprises accounted for 20 percent of total French industrial capacity.[3] In West Germany central government expenditures accounted for only 14 percent of gross national product; a much smaller percentage of the country's total industrial capacity was nationalized. Even the geography of

[2] *Economic Survey of Europe in 1958* (Geneva: United Nations, 1959), Chapter II, p. 15.
[3] Warren G. Baum, *The French Economy and the State* (Princeton, N. J.: Princeton University Press, 1958), p. 170.

the Community is not entirely persuasive. Its map reveals a gaping hole in the middle consisting of Switzerland, which constitutes a cultural and lingustic link among the three largest partners, France, Germany, and Italy. Nor were the trade ties among the six members of the Community at the time the Rome Treaty was drafted measurably stronger than those between the Community and other European countries. As of 1955, Austria and Switzerland relied on the six nations soon to form the Community for over 40 percent of their external trade;[4] the three southern European countries of Portugal, Turkey, and Greece relied upon them for 34 percent; and the Scandinavian countries relied upon them for 29 percent. In comparison, the internal trade of the six-member Community accounted for 31 percent of their total international trade. It can reasonably be inferred, therefore, that the EEC members were motivated not so much because the economic forces of integration operated on them more but rather because the political constraints obstructing such integration generally operated on them a great deal less. But, as I shall immediately endeavor to demonstrate, the constraints were present even among the six and were sufficiently strong to dictate the organizational form as well as the principal economic policies of the Community.

In theory the six member nations could have adopted any one of three broad policies in creating and operating an economic community: a policy of nonintervention toward the private business sector, which, by long

[4] *Economic Survey of Europe in 1956* (Geneva: United Nations), Chapter IV, p. 10.

tradition in all the member countries, would have meant acceptance of the cartel form of business organization; a variant of suprastate socialism, also a form of economic organization that most of the members, notably France, Germany, and Italy, had in their recent history developed to an advanced state; or competitive private capitalism not unlike that of the United States, the form least practiced and probably least understood in Western Europe.

In fact, however, if the Community was to take seriously its basic objective of a genuine economic community devoid of all internal barriers to trade and commerce, only the last two could be considered genuine alternatives. It is perfectly clear, and was clear to the architects of the EEC, that an intracommunity cartel could, through a policy of market division, zone pricing, and refusal to deal, offset many of the anticipated gains from the elimination of internal tariffs and quantitative restrictions. As was frequently stated by proponents of the Rome Treaty, the elimination of public barriers to trade would accomplish little unless private barriers were eliminated as well.

All this may explain why the Community rejected its historical and familiar form of permissive cartel organization for the private economy, but it does not explain why the Community, at least in principle, elected a policy of competitive private enterprise rather than one calling for an extension of the public economy through planning. The explanation for this, I believe, lies in the constraining force of vestigial nationalism. It is true, of course, that much analytical economics establishes a strong case for the superior efficiency and higher productivity of competitive private capitalism in comparison with either private cartelization or state socialism of the more bureaucratic variety. Europe in the mid-1950s attached a high premium to efficiency and productivity, as the proceedings of the Organization for European Economic Cooperation and the establishment of the various National Productivity Agency centers under the OEEC abundantly testify. The consistency of these broad economic goals with the logical constructions of traditional economic theory was not altogether overlooked by those entrusted with framing the policy foundations of the new Community. But there were also some factual arguments. Dr. Ludwig Erhard in his widely read book *Wholstand Für Alle* [5] had explained the "miracle" of West Germany in terms of that country's policies of fostering competitive enterprise. And in the decade preceding 1957 the conviction grew increasingly stronger in Western Europe that the extraordinary high standard of living reached by the United States was certainly to an important degree associated with, if not directly attributable to, its public policies supporting competitive enterprise.[6]

These considerations unquestionably influenced the ultimate decision of the Community members to accept in principle a policy calling for competitive enterprise. But the central consideration underlying the Community's decision in this regard was much more fundamental. An

[5] English edition: *Prosperity through Competition* (New York: Praeger, 1958).
[6] cf. O. D. K. Norbye, *Mission Report on Restrictive Business Practices in the United States,* Project No. 414, European Productivity Agency of the Organization for European Economic Cooperation (Paris: 1959).

economic integration plan calling for substantial government enterprise, or for substantial direct government control of privately operated enterprises—in short, central planning—would of necessity have required a strong central Community government. But a strong central Community government would in turn have required that the power of political prerogative otherwise exercised in Paris, Bonn, and Rome be, at least in substantial part, transferred to the Community government in Brussels. While, as I have argued, the decline of nationalism in the six countries was sufficient to unleash the economic forces operating in favor of an integrated economic community, nationalism had not, and still has not, declined to the point where the political policies of the six nations, especially their foreign policies, are accepted as coterminous with the supranational Community.

In contrast, economic integration sought through the policies of private competitive enterprise required only that the various national policies toward cartels and restrictive business practices be made compatible with those designed by the Commission in Brussels for the Community as a whole. In brief, while we may accept as valid the statement of Community spokesmen that in the formation and operation of the EEC political and economic affairs cannot be separated, acceptance of the policy of private enterprise competition afforded the most promising means for centralizing control over important economic policies in the hands of the Community's authorities in Brussels while leaving control over political affairs largely in the hands of the national governments back home.

The Community's acceptance of the principles of competitive enterprise and their attendant great reliance on the market economy explains in large part the disposition of certain issues that have arisen in the Community's brief history and has important implications for issues that will surely arise in the future. For example, virtually every nation in the world has empowered its central government to control, regulate, protect, and otherwise participate in the entrepreneurial function in agriculture. The six Common Market countries were, and still are, no exception; in each of them a heavy commitment to the agricultural sector was a serious matter of national economic and political policy. Clearly, to turn agriculture over to the market economy required a transfer of substantial control over national policy from the member countries to the authorities in Brussels. It is not surprising, therefore, that the substitution of Community for national policy has proceeded at a decidedly slower pace in the case of agriculture than in the case of industry generally.

Similarly, the Community's articulated reliance on competitive private enterprise may very well explain what in certain European circles is referred to as the anomaly of party positions in Great Britain. While I wish to make it clear that I am not an expert on British politics, I venture to suggest that the widely held view of the British Conservative Party is one reflecting an image of proper Victorian statesmen intent on preserving intact those traditions and institutions that can only be defined as properly British; the Labor Party, on the other hand, projects an image of qualified democratic "one worldliness"—a sort of Oxbridge internationale. Hence, the initiative taken by the Conservatives to lead Britain into the EEC over strong Labor Party objections appears contrary to expectations—until of course one is reminded that a market-governed economy, even a competitive market-governed economy, with little or no provision for central planning, ranks very low on the Labor Party's list of economic policy objectives.

The Community's basic policy of market competition also holds significant implications for the future membership of EEC. Every European nation outside the Soviet bloc, except Spain, has petitioned the EEC for full or limited membership. Greece is already an associate member under an agreement calling for a full customs-union status by November 1974. Associate membership for Turkey awaits only ratification by that country's parliament and those of the Community's members. It is generally believed that Austria will join the Community with as full participation as its peace treaty with the Soviet Union permits. It is clear, however, that the basic economic policy of the Community would undergo severe stress and strain in attempts to accommodate those applicants in which the state plays a much larger role in the economy than in the EEC. Compliance with articles 85 and 86 of the Rome Treaty, which set forth the Community's basic rules governing competition, and with the treaty's provisions calling for harmonization of the social legislation of member countries, would call for radical revision in the present national policies of such applicants as Sweden and Portugal, although for different reasons. It is equally clear that the Community could not readily accommodate nations that accept cartels of the type common in Europe prior to World War II. In sum, enlargement of the EEC's membership on the European continent, except possibly for the addition of Ireland, the United Kingdom, and Denmark, requires either that the applicant nations seriously revise their national economic policies, including concessions on the policy of nationalism itself, or that the EEC compromise its present delicate balance between economic unity and limited political nationalism.

The Economic Policies in Theory and in Practice Summary

Much of what I have said up to this point rests on two as yet unsupported assumptions:

1] The European Economic Community is, at least for the foreseeable future, an enduring economic and political fact of international life, and
2] The Community's proclaimed policies supporting market competition are in fact its operational policies; that is, it takes its articulated economic *Weltanschauung* seriously.

To comment with great assurance on the first of those assumptions requires an omniscience that obviously no one, least of all an American who has acquired a large fraction of his information from those heavily committed to the EEC as a going concern, possesses. Nevertheless, I am prepared to accept at face value President Walter Hallstein's assertion that "The European Economic Community is a political reality—now past the point of no return." President Hallstein was referring in his William L. Clayton Lectures at the Fletcher School of Law and Diplomacy to the member nations having in December 1961 cleared the last obstacle to economic integration: an agreement on a Community agricultural policy. But there is additional persuasive evidence that the EEC will endure, at least for some time to come: (1) Its progress toward economic and political integration in its six years of existence has exceeded the most optimistic expectations; (2) the progress toward integration has been identified as a causal factor in the unprecedented economic prosperity of the six member countries; (3) the Community survived its internal discord over the admission of Great Britain and the treaty banning the atmospheric testing of nuclear weapons; and (4) there is growing acceptance of the view, both inside and outside the member countries, that the Community is an economic, political, and historical necessity—no member confronts a feasible alternative.[7] The test of an institution's durability is its manifest capability of withstanding adversity as well as success. The European Economic Community has now survived half its planned transition period in the face of both.

Of course there are disintegrating forces that hold important implications for the long run viability of the EEC as presently constituted and administered. The two year *apertura a sinistra* in Italy shows no signs of narrowing.

---

[7] cf. President Walter Hallstein, "Face to Face with Historical Reality," *Bulletin from the European Community,* No. 57, October–November 1962, p. 6.

A significant further drift to the left in that country could create irreconcilable conflicts between its domestic economic policies and the "market economy" policies on which the Community has been built—and thus far has apparently prospered. Knowledgeable European students of the EEC also often generalize the potential Italian situation, pointing out that an extended period of large-scale unemployment, especially if accompanied by Socialist- and Labor-oriented party victories in other member countries, could easily lead to a resurgence of nationalism and its attendant disintegrating forces.[8] Labor, it is argued, is the last stronghold of nationalism in Western Europe; governments responsive to its demands are very likely to resort to traditional nationalistic economic policies as well as heavy doses of national planning to combat domestic unemployment.

It is the second proposition, however, the extent to which the Community actively pursues its acknowledged policy of integration through market competition, with which I am principally concerned. At the outset the essential ingredients of this policy must be defined in terms amenable to assessment, and the problems of assessment identified.

Limitations on the effective functioning of markets traditionally have arisen from two sources, governmentally imposed restrictions and private monopoly power. The traditional public policies for dealing with them are

---

[8] This argument was set forth most convincingly by Professor Edgar Salin of the Department of Economics, the University of Basil, in his lecture "The Economics of the European Common Market," Princeton University, October 29, 1963.

respectively the dismantling by government of restrictions it once imposed, usually trade liberalization, and the erection of legal institutions to mitigate the allocation-distorting effects of monopoly, usually anticartel or antitrust policy.

While both policies may be directed toward the objective of more efficient resource allocation within the relevant market area, they require totally different administrative procedures and must be assessed by totally different standards. Elimination of public trade barriers and restrictions merely requires that the government eliminate that which it once created. To be sure, in a democratic society the elimination of such public barriers may be unpopular with those made less well off in the dismantling process, and the action therefore may carry with it certain political risks. But in principle, the removal of publicly imposed trade restraints is simply the reversal of a previous governmental action.

In contrast, the amelioration of monopoly power and cartel arrangements in the private sector is a highly complex matter, as the now nearly seventy-five years of antitrust law administration in the United States abundantly testify. We not only have failed to develop an operational definition of monopoly that can be used to separate within tolerable limits the legal from the illegal but we are uncertain as to appropriate remedial action even after the definitional hurdle has been cleared. In the language of the well-known *Aluminum Company* decision, 33 percent of a relevant market does not constitute monopoly, 64 percent probably does not, and 90 percent almost certainly does; and in the equally imprecise language of the

National Lead case, we have no assurance that four competitors are better than two, or that six are better than four.

Moreover, policies toward public trade barriers and restrictions, in contrast with those toward their counterparts in the private sector, are susceptible to assessment in quantitative terms. A reduction in the import duty on commodity X of 50 percent, or a change in the quantitative restriction on the importation of commodity Y upward from twelve million to twenty-four million tons, is a measurable movement in the direction of trade liberalization. Progress in the dismantling of market power and restrictive business practices is often less discernible, and always less measurable.

The provisions of the Rome Treaty for the dismantling of both public and private trade barriers reflect these essential differences in the nature of the two complementary policies. The treaty establishes a timetable for the reductions in tariffs and quantitative restrictions among member countries, calling for their complete elimination within the Community at the end of the twelve-year transition period. Articles 85 and 86 of the treaty set forth the "Rules Governing Competition" in terms of much less definite objectives. Article 85, which resembles in scope and purpose Section 1 of our Sherman Act, prohibits certain interfirm agreements, concerted actions, and trade association activities likely to affect trade adversely or to impede the free play of competition within the Common Market. However, provisions are made for exempting such agreements and practices if a persuasive case can be made that they contribute to technical progress or greater efficiency in production or distribution. Article 86, the treaty's counterpart to Section 2 of our Sherman Act, prohibits one or more firms from taking unfair advantage of their dominant-firm position in ways that distort or impede intra-Community trade, but again the terms "unfair," "dominant," and what trade effects are in fact prohibited, are left undefined.

Any serious assessment of the Community's progress in the elimination of public and private trade restraints should take cognizance of the obvious disparity in standards by which progress must be judged, and must recognize also that in reducing public barriers the state deals with itself by eliminating those barriers it once created, whereas private cartels and monopoly positions have grown up in Europe not so much by government action but because governments did not act to prevent them. Their removal, therefore, requires more than simply the reversal of a previous policy; it requires the creation of an entirely new policy.

By all measurable standards the EEC has dismantled public barriers to trade at a remarkable pace.[9] By July 1963 internal tariffs on industrial products had been reduced to 40 percent of their 1957 levels, a point reached two full years ahead of schedule. Tariffs on the agreed-upon list of agricultural products have been reduced 40 percent; the original schedule called for a reduction by

[9] Much of the quantitative data appearing in the following pages may be found in a more extensive treatment of this subject in Jesse W. Markham, "Competition in the European Common Market," *Factors Affecting the United States Balance of Payments*, Joint Economic Committee, 87th Congress, 2d Sess., Committee Print (Washington, D. C.: 1962), pp. 135-56.

this time of 30 percent. By December 31, 1961, practically all quantitative restrictions on trade in industrial products had been abolished; the original timetable had scheduled their abolition by the end of 1969. By July 1, 1964, the Community will have moved well over halfway toward establishing a common external tariff, one of the very important features of the EEC that distinguishes it from the European Free Trade Association, and the issue on which the recent negotiations for the admission of Great Britain ostensibly broke down. By that date, the gap between national external tariffs and the common external tariff as of January 1958 will have been reduced by 60 percent. Export duties were completely eliminated by 1962.

Public barriers to intra-Community trade consist of much more than such visible obstacles as tariff walls and quantitative restrictions on the importation of goods and commodities. Restrictions on labor and enterprise mobility may offer as much interference to efficient resource allocation as tariffs. As of January 1958 such restrictions on the movement of labor and enterprise, and the attendant restrictions of the latter on capital mobility, were formidable. Labor moved from one member country to the other by the conventional instrument of the worker's permit granting the right of temporary residence. With six national jurisdictions governing corporate enterprise, a corporation in one member country seeking to conduct business in any of the other five confronted wide variations in corporate law, special restrictions, and cumbersome procedures imposed on foreign corporations, divergent and conflicting patent and corporate tax policies, even wide differences in the legal definition of a corporation. Collectively they imposed a substantial restriction on the mobility of capital and entrepreneurial, managerial, and technical resources.

The Community's progress toward greater labor mobility has received public notice largely because language and cultural barriers have turned out to be less important than anticipated. The American and European press has become well adjusted to the appellation "European" to designate that mobile young generation only a few years ago referred to as Dutch, French, Belgian, German, or Italian. But the economic effects of the new mobility far transcend the movement of youth across old national boundaries in Volkswagens, Renaults, and Vespas without even a brief pause for customs inspection. Thousands of Italian workers have migrated from southern Italy, where they were either unemployed or employed in occupations yielding a low marginal product, to fill the higher productivity employment opportunities in West Germany and elsewhere in the Community. The Common Market Commission has set January 1, 1964 as the deadline for abolishing the remaining national restrictions on the free mobility of labor, and a substantial beginning has been made on the harmonization of such institutions as social security, unemployment and retirement benefits, work rules, and minimum wages. More recently the Common Market Commission has also begun to implement its detailed proposals calling ultimately for complete mobility of business enterprises—usually referred to as "freedom of establishment."

Finally, EEC has taken steps toward the elimination of trade-distorting effects in the highly sensitive and important area of state-owned and state-operated enterprises. The area is sensitive because it is the most obvious point at which the prerogatives of national economic policy conflict with the new "market economy" *weltanschauung;* it is important because the manipulation of state subsidies and prices can offset the gains in Community-wide productivity and efficiency through the reallocation of resources attributable to the liberalization of tariffs and other intra-Community restrictions. Moreover, the opportunities to employ such subsidy manipulations in some of the member countries are numerous. In France, for example, the diverse list of state-owned or controlled enterprises includes, among others, coal mines, automobile plants, steel mills, aircraft manufacture, banks, insurance companies, a state tobacco monopoly, gas and electric companies, virtually all public transport systems, a radio and television corporation, the National Opera, Comédie Française, and stud farms for horses.[10] To "normalize" all these activities, an objective set forth in the Rome Treaty, calls for the ultimate pricing of the products and services of nationalized and state-controlled enterprises consistent with the market forces of supply and demand, which in operational terms means the eventual elimination of state subsidies having the effect of impairing competition in the Common Market. Since the principal motive for state intervention in mining, manufacturing, certain forms of transport, and agriculture has been either protection from imports or the promotion of exports, it is even conceivable that compliance with the Rome Treaty may eventually re-

[10] Baum, *op. cit.,* p. 169.

sult in a transfer of some of these enterprises from the public to the market economy—the *raison d'être* for state entrepreneurship will at that point have disappeared.

Normalization of state enterprises has not proceeded at a spectacular pace; but the pace has been discernible: On July 1, 1961, the Commission banned discriminatory transportation rates based on the origin or destination of goods; certain state monopolies—notably the French and Italian tobacco monopolies—have been deprived of much of the protection they once possessed; Volkswagen of Germany, long a state-owned enterprise, has recently been sold into private hands; and on a selective basis the trade distorting effects of state aid, subsidies, and turnover taxes have been mitigated, in some cases eliminated. In September 1963 the Common Market Commission even declared certain French agricultural subsidies incompatible with the Rome Treaty, and the means by which they were introduced in violation of the treaty's Article 93 requiring a "reasonable time" notification of the Commission for its formal opinion. The promptness of the Commission's action is as impressive as its substance. On August 7 and 12 France announced rebates of 50 percent of transport costs on the export of certain fruits and vegetables, and direct subsidies to certain agricultural producer associations, to become effective on August 15. The Commission's notice to the French government challenging the subsidies was rendered a few weeks thereafter.

In the removal of public barriers to trade the EEC is running impressively ahead of its original timetable. In the Community itself optimism over their complete removal by 1969, and possibly even by 1967, is running sufficiently high for the Commission to direct much of its planning effort in the second stage of the twelve-year transition period to what it calls an "action program" for full union—economic, social, and political union.[11] The draft proposals for the 1964–1968 program in this regard call for considerable merging of national policy into Community policy, even in such matters as foreign policy and defense. Plans have already been drawn up for extending in scope the Community's existing embryonic monetary and fiscal policy institutions. While the Rome Treaty did not provide for a common monetary and fiscal policy, it did call for coordination of national policies, and for the establishment of a European Investment Bank that already by the end of 1962 had made industrial development loans of 254.3 million dollars, of which the underdeveloped areas of Italy and France accounted respectively for 64 percent and 21 percent.[12] And in the first phase of the transition period the Community had taken one of the important steps toward a common monetary policy when it instituted the free convertibility of all member-country currencies. The Commission's recent memorandum proposes the establishment of a Monetary Council, eventually to become the central organ of a federal-type banking system.

It should not be inferred from all this that the EEC's task of removing the more visible public barriers to trade at the national level is completed. To return to the basic thesis of this essay, the greatest progress has occurred in

[11] See *Bulletin from the European Community*, no. 58, December 1962, p. 1.
[12] *Idem.*, no. 64, July–August 1963, p. 15.

areas where the reduction or elimination of public constraints has required the least encroachment on the member-countries' national prerogatives. It is not surprising, therefore, that national boundaries still divide the "common market" into six relevant geographical areas for a long list of agricultural products, certain state-trading monopolies, and enterprises with a long tradition of state subsidization. Normalization of these activities requires more from the state than simply the withdrawal of previously extended protection, as in the case of tariff reductions; it requires also the state's cessation of direct participation in the entrepreneurial function. It may be inconsistent with the Community's policies of competition that progress in these areas has not kept pace, but in view of the radical denationalization required, it is significant that the initial steps in this direction have been taken.

Private Restrictions and Anticartel Policies

In Europe, in contrast with the United States, cartels and monopoly traditionally have been regarded as neutral factors in the promotion of economic welfare. At the Twenty-sixth Conference of the Inter-Parliamentary Union held in London in 1930, a resolution stating that "cartels, trusts and other analogous combines are natural phenomena of economic life towards which it is impossible to adopt an entirely negative attitude" passed unanimously. As recently as 1956 the Belgian, Netherlands, and French delegates to the first OEEC conference of experts on restrictive business practices emphasized that, in their respective countrics, it was the abuse of monopoly power rather than its mere possession that was regarded as inimical to economic welfare. This basic philosophy is in sharp contrast to that of the United States as enunciated by the Supreme Court in the 1911 *Standard Oil* decision; the Court stated there that the Sherman Act does not condone good monopolies and forbid bad monopolies—it condemns them all; and makes monopoly effected through agreement a *per se* violation.

Articles 85 and 86 of the Rome Treaty go a considerable distance, but not all the way, toward the condemnation of monopoly. Article 85 deems as incompatible with the Common Market, and prohibits,

> any agreement between enterprises, and decisions by associations of enterprises and any concerted practices which are likely to (unfavorably) affect trade between the member states and which have as their object or result the prevention, restriction or distortion of competition within the Common Market.[13]

It specifically prohibits agreements on price fixing, other terms of sale, limitations on production, markets, technical developments, and investment, and the sharing of markets. However, the article may be declared by the Commission to be inapplicable to such agreements and concerted practices when they contribute to the improvement of production or distribution of goods or to the promotion of technical or economic progress, provided they neither impose on the enterprises concerned any restrictions not

[13] An English translation of the full text of articles 85 and 86 are appended to this essay.

indispensable to the attainment of these objectives nor enable such enterprises to eliminate competition in a substantial portion of the market. In short, while article 85 condemns cartels in the abstract as bad, it provides for exemptions of those whose effects in the judgment of the Commission may be good. But however similar to the traditional doctrine of the "neutrality" of the cartels this may on superficial examination appear, the difference is more than a matter of semantics. It should be noted that to qualify as a good cartel under the various exemptions, the cartel cannot impose on the enterprises concerned restrictions not indispensable to the beneficial objectives, nor can it eliminate competition in a substantial part of the relevant market.

Article 86 is more precise in what it encompasses but more obscure in what it in fact prohibits. Its concern is exclusively with a firm or group of firms that individually or collectively have a dominant position within the Common Market or a substantial part of it. Accordingly, it identifies monopoly power that inheres in a single firm or a highly concentrated oligopoly as a source of anticompetitive behavior. However, such market power is forbidden only when those who possess it use it to their advantage improperly. Such improper practices are identified in article 86 as the imposition of unequitable prices or trading conditions, the limitation of production or technical development to the prejudice of consumers, discrimination among customers that places any of them at a competitive disadvantage, and the use of tying contracts in goods having no connection with each other. Thus, article 86 seems to permit the mere possession of monopoly power, but prohibits the exercise of such power in ways that clearly reveal its possession.

At this point a brief description of the institutions and organization of the Community is necessary to an understanding of how articles 85 and 86 are, at least in theory, administered. The primary responsibility for the execution of all articles of the Rome Treaty is vested in the European Economic Community Commission. Its nine members, on taking office, become independent of member states and responsible only to the Community as a whole. It is empowered to call member-countries and enterprises to account when they fail to comply with the provisions of the treaty. In this respect it can be said to resemble any one of the independent regulatory commissions of the United States, although its jurisdiction encompasses a much wider range of activities. A second function of the Commission is to make proposals to the Council of Ministers—a council made up of one minister from each of the six member countries. Such proposals require approval of the Council of Ministers before they can be made effective. The "qualified majority" rule applies in most matters where the treaty requires that the Commission make proposals to the Council of Ministers; that is, a minimum of twelve out of a possible total of seventeen votes must be cast in favor of the proposal.[14] A unanimous vote is required to modify a proposal of the Commission and in exceptional cases that bear significantly on national sovereignty. The Commission and the

[14] When the "qualified majority" rule applies, France, Germany, and Italy each have four votes, the Netherlands and Belgium each have two votes, and Luxembourg has one vote.

Council of Ministers are generally regarded as jointly comprising the decision-making agency of the EEC.

The final authority on the interpretation of the Rome Treaty, as well as the treaties establishing the European Coal and Steel Community and Euratom, is vested in the seven-member Court of Justice—the Community's Supreme Court. Its verdicts arising out of litigation between member nations and all other legal persons are directly enforceable by the member nations' competent authorities. To date, no order of the court has been defied.

In view of their brief history the EEC's anticartel policies as spelled out in articles 85 and 86 must be assessed much more in terms of their prospective interpretation than their past application. While the articles were written into the Rome Treaty as rules of law and not simply as statements of principle, they were held in virtual abeyance until the Community's Council, acting on a Commission proposal, issued its first regulation governing competition in the Common Market on December 30, 1961, to become effective on March 13, 1962. Prior to March 13, 1962, the Commission and the Council considered the articles as the equivalent of internal law, and therefore self-executing; that is, they were to be administered by the competent authorities in each of the member countries. However, only three of the member countries, West Germany, France, and the Netherlands, had already enacted legislation controlling restrictive practices by the time the Rome Treaty became effective, and the laws of these countries differed considerably among themselves. The period from January 1, 1958 to March 13, 1962 was, therefore, for all practical purposes an interregnum, during which time the competent national authorities exercised articles 85 and 86 only seven times, all of which were *Bundeskartellamt* decisions, and all of which concerned exemptions.[15]

The Council's March 13, 1962 regulation had as its main purposes the assurance that articles 85 and 86 would be uniformly applied throughout the Community, clarification of the law for all parties concerned, and provision of the necessary procedures and powers for the Commission to pursue an effective anticartel policy. It leaves the application of articles 85 and 86 in the hands of the competent authorities in member countries only until the Commission assumes jurisdiction, at which time the authority of member states is vacated. However, only the Commission is competent to grant exemptions. To qualify for exemption, parties to an agreement must notify the Commission of its details, which may be published by the Commission so that interested third parties can file their objections. Publication by the Commission generally implies that the Commission intends to grant the requested exemption unless objections by third parties or the discovery of new facts leads to a contrary decision.

The 1962 regulation empowers the Commission to make the necessary investigations of agreements and enterprise activities, to issue cease and desist orders, and to impose fines of from one hundred to one million units of account for violation. To encourage timely compliance with the Commission's decisions, fines may be imposed at the rate

[15] Norbert Koch, "The European Economic Community," *Patent, Trademark and Copyright Journal of Research and Education*, Vol. 6, 1962, Conference Number, p. 99.

of from fifty to one thousand units of account per day of delay.

Proceedings under the EEC's new regulations provide too meager a past from which to assess the present or predict the future of the Community's policies toward private restraints on intra-Community trade. As of August 1, 1963, the Commission had initiated fifty-one proceedings under articles 85 and 86.[16] The details of the proceedings have not yet been made public. In July 1963 the Commission published its first details on applications for "negative clearance." The applications were made by two French firms, both involving exclusive dealing agreements with firms in nonmember countries. Such publication, as already pointed out, implies Commission approval. The two cases are regarded as important largely because the EEC Commission has been notified of several hundred exclusive dealing agreements between member- and nonmember-country enterprises, and the July 1963 publications can be considered as setting a precedent.

The "Rules of Competition" in the EEC still lack the predictability that usually accompanies frequent application of law in a variety of specific cases. Nevertheless, in the broad sweep of recent economic history there are developments that collectively add up to an unmistakable trend in the Community nations, and in Western Europe generally, toward a growing mistrust of their traditional cartel policy and a perceptible trend toward an insistence on reasonably free and open competition. The pace at which antitrust legislation has sprung up on the European

[16] *European Community*, No. 68, October 1963, p. 6.

scene is itself significant. As of 1950 there was not a single agency in all of Western Europe seriously exercising control over monopoly and restraints of trade. By 1960 only four countries were without such agencies; in two of these articles 85 and 86 were self-executing, and in another legislation was before parliament for consideration. Spain, the remaining country, is not listed in the various international legislative guides as having such legislation. To be sure, some of the legislation is still to be exercised; the Netherlands' law, in its present form, is still a broad economic rule of reason; and the only law on the entire continent of Europe concerned directly with the prevention of structural monopoly, as distinct from restricting the exercise of monopoly power, is article 66 of the treaty establishing the European Coal and Steel Community. That article provides that any transaction creating a concentration in the Common Market for coal and steel must be approved by the High Authority. Approval must be granted provided the proposed concentration does not give the enterprises involved the power to fix prices, control or restrict production or distribution, or to prevent effective competition in a substantial part of the market. In its first ten years of administering article 66, the High Authority approved forty-eight concentrations and formally denied none; however, it has modified several proposals and has prevented at least one large merger by imposing sufficiently restrictive conditions to induce withdrawal of the application.

The four national policies toward monopoly and cartels in the EEC (Luxembourg and Italy still have such legislation before their respective parliaments) are of importance for several reasons: they reflect the attitudes toward anticompetitive practices at the national level; they govern such practices until the European Economic Commission establishes jurisdiction; and the authorities that administer them are responsible for administering the Commission's rulings and the decisions of the Court of Justice. However, for some time to come the various national policies are likely to be of greater importance than these specific areas of application would suggest. The EEC, in contrast with the United States, has just begun the long and difficult process of defining interstate (intracommunity) and intrastate (intranational) trade. Until such definitions are developed there will always be the question of whether the Commission or the competent national authorities have jurisdiction in certain borderline cases.

While the national policies represented in the EEC are diverse in substantive content, they lend themselves to several useful generalizations.[17] In all four nations, except for certain provisions of the French and West German laws, the test of legality applied to agreements among firms is their actual or potential adverse effect on the "public interest" rather than on "competition"; and the test applied to monopoly is the abuse of market power

[17] A more detailed analysis of national anticartel policies in the EEC may be found in the author's monograph, "Competition in the European Common Market," *Factors Affecting the United States Balance of Payments*, Joint Economic Committee, Subcommittee on International Exchange and Payments, 87th Congress, 2d Session (Washington, D. C.: 1962), pp. 137–55.

rather than its mere possession. The Belgian and Dutch laws are set forth in these terms, although the latter provides in addition that all agreements and trade-association decisions affecting competition, except individual resale-price-maintenance agreements and agreements involving markets outside the Netherlands, must be registered with the Economics Ministry. The Dutch law leaves wide discretion in the hands of the Ministry for the disposition of such agreements as well as for the disposition of acts by dominant enterprises.

The French law, reflecting the French government's concern over postwar inflation and industrial rehabilitation, imposes relatively strict prohibitions on price-fixing agreements that tend to raise prices and is comparatively tolerant toward agreements that promote efficiency and market rationalization. It specifically forbids refusals to sell, price increases not cost-justified, conditioning the sale of one good on the purchase of a stipulated quantity of another, and the fixing of minimum prices. The last prohibition covers resale-price maintenance of all kinds and horizontal-price maintenance enforced by either a cartel or a dominant firm. The French law also prohibits

> every concerted action, convention, combine, express or implied, or trade coalition in any form, which has the object or may have the effect of interfering with full competition by hindering the reduction of production costs or selling prices or by encouraging an artificial increase in prices.[18]

[18] *Guide to Legislation on Restrictive Business Practices,* OECD, November 1961, France, Section 1, p. 4.

However, exemption is made where the effect is to further economic progress by extending markets or by rationalization or specialization. The French principle of prohibitions with exemptions requires that the activities of each combine, agreement, and dominant enterprise be examined on a case-by-case basis, since the law establishes no presumption of illegality until the grounds for exemption have been analyzed. But infringement of the law, once the determination is made, is a criminal offense that in theory is subject to severe penalties—prison terms up to five years and fines up to six million new francs. In fact, however, the government generally seeks voluntary compliance rather than relief through court action.

The West German law against restraints of competition enacted in 1957 is the most comprehensive statute of its kind. In terms of substantive provisions it is also the national policy most akin to articles 85 and 86 of the Rome Treaty. It prohibits horizontal agreements but provides for two important classes of exemptions: agreements concerned with rebates, general delivery terms, exports, and uniform application of standards registered with the Federal Cartel Authority (*Bundeskartellamt*) but not challenged within three months; and application for the Authority's express authorization under any of the special provisions for exemption that include, among others, agreements necessitated by a crisis, the public interest, or a special economic situation, rationalization agreements, and export and import agreements. The act also prohibits vertical agreements except for the resale price maintenance of branded goods in open price competition. However, the details of the agreement must be filed with the Federal Cartel Authority in order to qualify for the resale-price-maintenance exemption. The Authority can prohibit the abuses of market power by dominant firms, and while it is not empowered to take action against mergers, all those involving as much as twenty percent of a relevant market must be reported to the Authority.

The parade of national and supranational antitrust policies growing up in Western Europe over the past decade scarcely adds up to a blueprint for effective competition by American standards, but before we on this side of the Atlantic judge the EEC policies toward private monopoly too harshly we should remind ourselves of Judge Wyzanski's dictum laid down in the *United Shoe Machinery* case sixty-three years after the passage of the Sherman Act:

> In antitrust matters the courts have been given unusual power. They would not have been given, nor allowed to keep this power, if they used it with the surgical ruthlessness proposed by economists committed to the vigorous pursuit of workable competition.

To continue the allegory, the antitrust surgeons of Western Europe are still serving their internships. And while the laws under which they work do not contemplate an eventual state of workable competition on all sides, they comprise a major step away from the cartelized economies of the recent past.

Furthermore, the logic of the case argues pursuasively that in their initial phases the Community's policies for eliminating public trade barriers are capable of promoting a reasonably competitive industrial base more expeditiously than its antitrust policies, however vigorously the latter are administered. In fact, a plausible case can be made that the dismantling of public barriers must have proceeded to an advanced stage before an antitrust policy against privately held monopoly power can be effectively pursued. All members of the Community are, by all indexes of size familiar to students of the American economy, small economies. In the language of Adam Smith, division of labor in all of them is limited by the extent of the market. The sketchy available data on industrial structure suggests that the level of concentration at the national level in most manufacturing industries is high, although not always higher than that in the same industries in the United States.

The automobile industry illustrates in a striking fashion how the amalgamation of the six national markets into a common market through reductions in public trade barriers can greatly reduce the level of market concentration: Prior to the creation of the EEC the four largest motor vehicle producers in West Germany—Volkswagen, Opel, Daimler-Benz, and Ford-Werke—accounted for 76 percent of the total national output of motor vehicles. Volkswagen alone accounted for 36 percent. In France the four largest accounted for 94 percent, with Renault alone accounting for nearly 39 percent. The level of concentration in Italy was as high as that in France, while the three Benelux countries together had a single automobile assembly plant. In the combined six-country market the four largest producers account for only 45 percent, and the largest firm, Volkswagen, for only 15 percent. This comparison is not to imply that before the EEC was formed the automobile industries in each member country operated as tightly-knit oligopolies enjoying complete protection from competition from other member countries. However, the competitive pressures exerted on the structural oligopoly in each was surely much weaker than it now is. The trade in automobiles between France and Germany in 1957 amounted to approximately 3,000 vehicles, or to a fraction of 1 percent of each country's domestic production, and faced an *ad valorem* import duty of 30 percent in France and 32 percent in Germany. In the automobile industry, and in other industries, the use of antitrust policy to maintain competition may well require as a first step the creation of market competition through the removal of public barriers.

Summary

The concern of this essay has been the political economy of the European Economic Community. Its focus has been on the public policies that give the Community its direction and adhesion. These policies, as I have outlined them, point unmistakably toward a substantial enlargement of the role of the market economy. And while this rebirth of competitive enterprise in Europe may, as I have argued, have been dictated by the political constraint of a waning but not yet expired adherence to nationalism, the event does not for this reason lose any of its significance for the United States. From its early decartelization plan for Germany under occupation, through the decade of the Organization for European Economic Cooperation, down to the formation of the EEC itself, the United States has urged upon Europe the economic philosophy of private competitive enterprise with reasonably effective containment of monopoly and restrictive business practices. Simultaneously, it has urged on Europe that it form a more perfect union than the loosely-knit association of European nations in the OEEC. The European Common Market at least in part fulfills both of these foreign policy objectives, and it is unquestionably far better that the fulfillment is more attributable to economic and political necessity than to our insistence.

Finally, in keeping with the current high propensity of economists to quantify their analysis, one would like to conclude with the pronouncement that the EEC is, say, within 70 percent of attaining its objectives, or at least that it is responsible for a large fraction of its 100 percent increase in internal trade, its 9 per cent annual rate of growth in industrial production, and its enviable state of virtual full employment, registered between January 1958 and December 1962. Attempts at such quantification have thus far been unsuccessful. Perhaps this does not really matter. The significant fact is that those who speak for the Common Market attribute much of its measurable performance to its new policies, and as long as they do the new policies will be exercised and very likely expanded. This suggests that in the future the world will contain two large and viable adherents to the market economy. Two may not be many, but it represents a tremendous percentage increase over the number in existence only a short decade ago. But the EEC experience may be of even much greater long run economic and political significance. When viewed in the context of a world that seems intent on creating common markets, free trade areas, and trade blocks in an era of flourishing nationalism, it may have identified a new historic role for the concept of the competitive market economy.

Appendix on Rules Governing Competition in the European Economic Community Treaty [1]

ARTICLE 85

1. The following shall be deemed to be incompatible with the Common Market and shall hereby be prohibited, namely: any agreement between enterprises, any decisions by associations of enterprises and any concerted practices which are likely to (unfavorably) affect trade between the Member States and which have as their object or result the prevention, restriction or distortion of competition within the Common Market, in particular those consisting in

- a] the direct or indirect fixing of purchase or selling prices or of any other trading conditions;
- b] the limitation or control of production, markets, technical development or investment;
- c] market-sharing or the sharing of sources of supply;
- d] the application to parties to transactions of unequal terms in respect of equivalent supplies, thereby placing them at a competitive disadvantage; or

[1] English translation provided by EEC office, Brussels.

e] the subjecting of the conclusion of a contract to the acceptance by a party of additional supplies which, either by their nature or according to commercial usage, have no connection with the subject of such contract.

2. Any agreements or decisions prohibited pursuant to this Article shall be null and void.

3. Nevertheless, the provisions of paragraph 1 may be declared inapplicable in the case of:

—any agreements or classes of agreements between enterprises,

—any decisions or classes of decisions by associations or enterprises, and

—concerted practices or classes of concerted practices which contribute to the improvement of the production or distribution of goods or to the promotion of technical or economic progress while reserving to users an equitable share in the profit.

a] neither impose on the enterprises concerned any restrictions not indisposable to the attainment of the above objectives;
b] nor enable such enterprises to eliminate competition in respect of a substantial proportion of the goods concerned.

ARTICLE 86

To the extent to which trade between any Member States may be (unfavorably) affected thereby, action by one or more enterprises to take improper advantage of a dominant position within the Common Market or within a substantial part of it shall be deemed to be incompatible with the Common Market and shall hereby be prohibited.

Such improper practices may, in particular, consist in:

a] the direct or indirect imposition of any inequitable purchase or selling prices or of any other inequitable trading conditions;
b] the limitation of production, markets or technical development to the prejudice of consumers;
c] the application to parties to transactions of unequal terms in respect of equivalent supplies, thereby placing them at a competitive disadvantage; or
d] the subjecting of the conclusion of a contract to the acceptance, by a party of additional supplies which, either by their nature or according to commercial usage, have no connection with the subject of such contract.

2.

THE AMERICAN CORPORATION IN THE COMMON MARKET

Charles E. Fiero
Vice President
Chase Manhattan Bank

Introduction

I am delighted to have this chance to talk to you today about the role of the American corporation in the Common Market because I feel that some important issues have arisen about this role that need to be discussed. United States corporate subsidiaries in Europe have, in a sense, been under attack. On this side of the Atlantic they are accused of contributing to our balance of payments deficit, of exporting job opportunities, and of making it more difficult to increase U. S. exports. In Europe, U. S. subsidiaries are accused of being insensitive to the needs of the European economies and of exercising excessive control in industries that some identify with national prestige.

I have a great deal of confidence in the reasonable attitude of the great majority of Americans and Europeans about these matters. I know that the initial attitude to which I refer reflects a relatively small segment of opinion. And I am deeply aware that we must not consider all changes in attitude toward U. S. investments—many of which are very reasonable—as an attack on the concept of foreign investments.

Yet there has been much evidence—in the form of statements by public officials, newspaper reports, and in the form of actual and proposed legislation in this country and in Europe—to show that misconceptions exist concerning the role of direct U. S. investments in Europe. I believe these misconceptions may have results that are damaging to both our economy and to the economy of Europe.

For this reason I propose to evaluate the over-all effect of U. S. subsidiaries in Europe and to deal with the many misconceptions about their size, their impact, and their role. First, I would like to review the main facts regarding direct U. S. investments in Europe. I shall then attempt to answer three questions: What is the impact of direct U. S. investments on our balance of payments? Then, what impact does the U. S. corporation have on the European economic and social environment? And, finally, what impact do U. S. investments in Europe have on the philosophy and structure of the U. S. corporation?

U. S. Balance of Payments

Let me begin by trying to put direct U. S. investments into historical perspective. I think it is useful to remember that the flow of these investments is but a part—although an important part—of one of the truly great postwar phenomena, namely, the immense and entirely unprecedented outpouring of real and financial wealth from the United States to other nations of the Free World.

On the one hand, the U. S. government has spent an average of almost six billion dollars a year since 1945 in the form of grants and credits used for economic development and reconstruction and in the form of military equipment and services overseas. This massive outflow of nearly six billion dollars a year is one measure of the greatly expanded role of the United States in world affairs since World War II. What has this meant? For the United States as a nation, it has meant that in the space of a generation this country has moved from an essentially parochial and passive international posture to one that is broad-ranged and active. It has meant the assumption of leadership in marshalling the resources of the Free World in defense against intended encroachments of the Communist powers; it has meant large expenditures to help restore the basis for a free and independent Europe after the war; and it has meant a continuing struggle with the problem of spurring economic development in the emerging nations of the Free World. All this is now part of our living history.

On the other hand, private foreign investments have averaged nearly two billion dollars a year—half of which has been in the form of direct investments in overseas enterprises. I mention it here to point up a parallel development in American corporations, for they, too, have taken on new responsibilities and developed new attitudes toward the world outside our national frontiers. This is vividly demonstrated in the behavior and outlook of our most active and forward-looking companies. These companies have recognized that the U. S. market is only one—though still the most important one, to be sure—among many markets that can be profitably tapped. And, they have long since recognized that the United States is only one of many possible locations for new investments. As a result of this new attitude we have seen a growing stream of capital flow out of this country setting up production capacity overseas nearer the foreign markets, in order to do business from a position that is less vulnerable to trade barriers or high production costs in this country.

I shall have more to say about this change in the attitude and character of U. S. corporations overseas in a moment. But first I must deal with the criticisms mentioned earlier regarding their impact on the U. S. balance of payments.

Huge expenditures overseas for defense, economic aid, and investments have been a significant cause of our balance of payments deficit over the last decade. Even though much of the outflow consisted of actual goods and services, a substantial amount was in the form of dollar payments that could be accumulated or spent in other countries. The resulting net dollar outflow averaged about 1.7 billion a year between 1950 and 1957. Then, after a small surplus in 1957, we have experienced deficits averaging over 3 billion dollars a year. Of course, the moderate deficits before 1957 did not cause any concern primarily because they generally did not involve sizable gold outflows, but rather resulted in an accumulation of foreign-owned dollar assets—U. S. Treasury bills and bank deposits—in this country. These dollar assets provided much-needed dollar liquidity to the accumulating countries and thus helped to stabilize the international payments mechanism by increasing the world's modest supply of foreign exchange reserves.

But since 1958 a large part of the recurring U. S. deficits was paid in gold and the total outflow of gold in the space of the last five and a half years amounted to some 7 billion dollars.

Because this is a serious problem, and because private capital flowing out of the country is a debit item in the U. S. balance of payments, it has been suggested that we should slow down the outflow of capital in order to improve our over-all international payments position. Last year, for example, the administration presented a bill that would have required U. S. companies to pay a tax on the income from overseas subsidiaries in the industrially developed countries regardless of whether the income was remitted to the parent company as income or not. One of the aims of the proposed tax was to help stem the balance of payments outflow.

But clearly, any such proposal to retard private direct investment outflows rests on a superficial analysis of the facts. It disregards the return flow of dividends, interest, royalties, and management fees. To illustrate, the postwar outflow of direct investment capital has totaled about 15 billion dollars, while the return flow of income from dividends, interest, and fees from investments exceeded the capital outflow by more than 8 billion dollars.

Two main arguments are usually advanced in support of capital controls. First, a substantial portion of the income from foreign investments arises from the extractive industries in the less developed countries, not in the highly industrial nations of Europe. Therefore, the U. S. should have a double policy—one of "control" for developed industrialized nations and one of "noncontrol" or lesser control for underdeveloped nations. And second, while a reduction of direct investment outflows to the developed industrial nations now might work against our balance of payments in the long run, it would certainly help in the short run because most of the income returning to the United States is generated by already existing overseas enterprises rather than from very recent investments.

One should be able to prove out these two arguments by analyzing the flows of payments that arise from U. S. subsidiary operations in Western Europe. The facts, however, do not support the case for capital controls. In 1962, for example, direct U. S. capital outflows to Europe amounted to 811 million dollars, while dividend income from European investments totaled 520 million in the same year, and royalties and management fees another 200 million. This leaves an apparent net deficit on the direct investment account of less than 90 million dollars, surely too small an amount to be declared a major culprit in our balance of payments dilemma.

The argument that controls would temporarily benefit our balance of payments may also be fallacious even in the short run. One immediate result of investment controls could be the emergence of a black market for investment funds in Europe, as future subsidiary profits would not be remitted but lent out to other companies that wish to make investments in Europe. Conceivably this reduction in the flow of dividends would substantially offset any gain. On these grounds, therefore, the case for a tax that would slow down or halt direct investments in Europe does not appear very strong.

However, the problem of estimating the total or overall effect of direct investments on the U. S. balance of payments is very complex. And since these issues are a bit involved I shall only summarize some of them.

First, a portion of direct U. S. investments really are shipments of capital goods, but appear in the balance of payments both as an outflow of capital and a receipt for an export, although no financial flow took place. A casual reading would lead one mistakenly to assume that such capital exports affected our balance of payments.

Second, U. S. subsidiaries tend to buy some of their raw materials and semimanufactured components from the United States, exports that often could not be made without manufacturing and assembling facilities abroad.

Third, U. S. subsidiaries seldom produce the entire product range of their parent company. Therefore, they provide an important entry into the European markets for the expansion of sales of United States-made products that are not produced in Europe. Some companies report such sales over the years to have more than exceeded the initial dollar capital transfer from the United States for new investments.

While it is impossible to place an exact value on U. S. exports to Europe that are directly attributable to direct U. S. investments, the figure could be quite high. The Department of Commerce conducted a survey which showed that in 1960 exports from a sampling of U. S. companies to their European subsidiaries amounted to more than 500 million dollars, while imports into the United States from the same subsidiaries amounted to less than 100 million—yielding a net balance in favor of the United States of over 400 million dollars.

Thus in 1962, U. S. companies received about 520 million dollars in dividend income and 200 million in fees from their European subsidiaries. I believe it is entirely possible that the subsidiaries were directly responsible for at least 400 million dollars of net U. S. exports. This balance of payment credit of altogether 1 billion, 120 million dollars would exceed by a substantial margin the 811 million dollars of direct investment outflow recorded for that year.

Of course there is another side to the story. One must wonder if sales from U. S. controlled plants in Europe may have reduced U. S. exports or retarded their growth. A Department of Commerce survey showed that in 1962 U. S. manufacturing companies with direct investments abroad sold almost three times more electrical machinery, rubber products, paper, and chemicals from their foreign plants than they exported in that year. But clearly, most of these subsidiary sales could not have been made from the U. S. The reasons for this were emphasized rather effectively by John Dunning, who some years ago conducted a survey of U. S. subsidiaries in the United Kingdom. Among his findings he established that American companies who set up plants in the United Kingdom were not able to compete in that market from plants in the United States. This was true for three reasons:

first, because of transportation costs, which a majority of the surveyed firms estimated would increase their costs by more than 10%; second, because of tariffs, which were said to add 10 percent or more to the costs of over 75 percent of products exported to the United Kingdom by U. S. concerns; third, because of the fact that three out of every five U. S. subsidiaries stated that they could produce more cheaply in the United Kingdom than could their parent company in the United States.

Certainly for all these reasons it is difficult to conceive that American companies could have maintained their European markets through exporting. Rising competition from domestic corporations, tariffs, transportation charges, and higher production costs would have made them noncompetitive. No definite conclusion can be reached as to what extent sales from foreign plants replaced U. S. exports. However, it seems probable that for the most part products sold by U. S. subsidiaries in Europe did not reduce U. S. exports, but instead created new sales opportunities. As you can see, I am unable to be concerned about the over-all impact of American investments in Europe on the U. S. balance of payments— in fact, I believe that the total effect is a positive one.

Yet any analysis of the balance-of-payments impact on U. S. investment in Europe must come up with an even better evaluation for future years. Then, more U. S. investments will be financed out of retained earnings and depreciation allowances of U. S. subsidiaries abroad— a method of financing that does not involve an outflow of capital from the United States. Furthermore, the return flow of dividends, royalties, and management fees should grow as even larger investment totals in Europe generate greater earnings. On the other hand, the dependence of U. S. subsidiaries on goods from the United States may diminish. Yet over-all, the U. S. balance of payments must be expected to benefit from direct U. S. investments in Europe.

The second argument against direct U. S. foreign investments—one that is sometimes put forward by labor unions—is that when U. S. companies establish productive facilities overseas they are in effect exporting jobs, causing unemployment in this country to rise. There is no hard and fast evidence on this issue, but it seems to me that if there has been an unemployment effect due to foreign investments, it has been relatively minor. Indeed, it could be argued that U. S. direct investments have increased employment in this country—although, again, very slightly. I shall simply make three points briefly:

First, most U. S. companies that set up or expand production overseas do so to take advantage of conditions that would otherwise be availed of by foreign companies. Thus an export of U. S. capital designed to develop basic resources in order to serve markets here that would otherwise be served by companies from other nations is more likely to expand production here than to reduce it. This may even be true in the case of manufactured products. For instance, whether U. S. companies invested heavily in automobile production in Europe or not, European manufacturers would have increased their exports to the U. S. Also, European firms would gradually have taken over the bulk of the European market.

Clearly, in the great majority of cases, U. S. automotive production facilities overseas have been an outgrowth of particularly favorable market and factor-cost conditions. If U. S. companies had not taken advantage of it others would have done so. With the U. S. company doing it, however, we benefit, inasmuch as spare parts and replacements are standardized and hence manufactured in the United States.

Furthermore, if U. S. companies had chosen not to invest at all, many jobs would not have been created. It is true that an overseas investment may not create immediate need for production personnel in the U. S., although even this is debatable. It does, however, clearly create new jobs on the management level and requires more clerical and research personnel in the U. S. The effect thus is to shift employment demand to the administrative area. This has had the tendency both to upgrade the quality of the demand and increase the range of opportunities for American administrative personnel. While I have not seen any figures in this area, if there is any truth to Parkinson's law, one can only conclude that such demand results in a strong employment multiplier. But regardless of whether Mr. Parkinson has hit upon a valid social theorem, the world-wide expansion of U. S. business has undoubtedly created many new jobs and opened up many new opportunities for professional business managers as well as for clerical personnel.

Also, one must remember that the level of employment in this country is only to a small extent related to the U. S. level of exports. This is so because exports account for less than 5 percent of total production in the United States. Thus a 10 percent drop in exports would have about the same impact on employment as a drop of one half percent in gross national product. This is extremely small in comparison with normal year-to-year changes in GNP. Nonetheless, even a small change in our over-all trade picture may have a substantial effect on a given company or industry, just as the changes associated with economic progress often involve serious problems for some industries that do not share in the general advance. Indeed, in both international and domestic trade there are fluctuations and adjustments within industries—which are part of the price we pay to achieve the flexibility and vigor associated with growing economies.

If I have been at all successful in the discussion so far, I have shown that U. S. direct investments in Europe have neither weakened our own economy nor our over-all balance of payments. Instead, they have broadened the base of American business, which in turn made possible the continuation of international business by circumventing trade barriers and by taking advantage of international cost differences.

U. S. Subsidiaries in Europe

I should like to turn now to a different set of problems, namely, the problems that have arisen out of a gradual change in attitudes within Europe toward U. S. subsidiaries and U. S. direct investments.

I must emphasize at the outset that I believe the general attitude of European governments and the business community toward U. S. corporate activity there is on balance favorable. After World War II, American companies contributed significantly in capital and technology to the Herculean task of reconstruction. This contribution has not been forgotten. But, by the same token, the problem is different now. While Europe still needs new capital and new technical resources to achieve the rapid growth goals it has set for itself, the need is more selective and less urgent. Europe has emerged with great economic strength, capable of drawing forth a large flow of internally generated savings and producing an important measure of technical advance. Under these circumstances, Europeans have begun to look at U. S. investments from a new vantage point—a point of nationalistic self-interest that was unthinkable during the reconstruction period. It is not surprising, therefore, that on first look some fears should be expressed: fear that the U. S. companies will dominate industries in a way damaging to the interests of the host country, fear of the sheer competitive power of many U. S. corporations, fear that the balance of payments problem associated with servicing the growing volume of U. S. investments will become excessively burdensome. I believe such apprehensions are normal, if somewhat exaggerated. Also, this new attitude does not give proper weight to the contributions that U. S. investments are making. I should like to discuss, one by one, the problems that appear to concern some of our European host nations.

The most persistent of all European complaints about the inflow and growth of direct U. S. investments center on the allegedly increasing degree of U. S. domination in European industries.

Perhaps we can get a better focus on this problem if we remember that the book value of American investments in Europe, at the end of 1962, totaled roughly 8.8 billion dollars. Of this total, 3.8 billion was invested in Great Britain, while much smaller amounts, 1.5 billion and 1 billion, were invested in Germany and France, respectively. This means, by the rough measures available, that U. S. companies controlled between 2 percent and 5 percent of European industry. A more exact estimate can be made of the U. S. share of the annual net fixed capital investment of business enterprises in Europe. In 1961, for example, total business investment in plant and equipment in the six Common Market countries and the United Kingdom was 30.9 billion dollars, while plant and equipment expenditures of U. S. subsidiaries amounted to less than 1.3 billion. This means that investments in U. S. subsidiaries were less than 4 percent of the total. Clearly, these investment shares cannot be said to constitute economic dominance.

Another way to demonstrate the relatively small share of European industry held by U. S. subsidiaries is to compare total sales of U. S. manufacturing subsidiaries in the Common Market and in the United Kingdom with over-all sales of manufacturing industries in these countries. The evidence points again to relative unimportance of U. S. subsidiaries. In 1962, U. S. subsidiaries sold 11.2 billion dollars of manufacturing output, which amounts, according to my calculation, to between 2.5 percent and

3.5 percent of total manufacturing sales in the Common Market and the United Kingdom—a small share indeed.

How good are these measures? Anybody familiar with corporate accounting realizes that measures of book value are in general very inadequate. On the other hand, expenditures for plant and equipment have been reliably recorded for U. S. subsidiaries, while the gross national product component "net fixed capital investment of business in plant and equipment" for the European economies are equally good technical estimates. But since net investment figures are smaller than expenditure figures by the amount of depreciation, I am reasonably confident that the share of U. S. subsidiaries is less than 4 percent. Also, the comparison of plant and equipment expenditures is backed up by the relative measure of sales of manufacturing industries. While total European sales are estimated from GNP data of manufacturing output, and hence subject to considerable error, there is no doubt that U. S. subsidiary sales are less than 5 percent of total sales in the Common Market and the United Kingdom. For the United Kingdom by itself, U. S. subsidiary sales may reach 7 percent of total British manufacturing sales, the percent share for Germany about equals the combined measure, while that of Italy and France is below 3 percent.

Again, these measures point to a relatively small share for U. S. subsidiaries in the major European economies, and this statistic should be kept in mind. On the other hand, in some industries—for example, automobiles in Germany, office machines in the United Kingdom, and even biscuits in France, U. S. subsidiaries have substantial shares of the respective national markets. Yet, I think it is fair to ask what harmful effects such selective concentration of U. S. companies may have on the European economies. In what way may it be to the detriment of the respective European nation and its citizens to have its electronic computers or its automobiles produced by companies that are owned by American corporations?

Clearly, American corporations are attracted to the European markets because of good profits and favorable prospects for sales expansion. And in most cases, U. S. firms invest because they possess some special competitive advantage in the form of a new product or a new technology. Some such advantage is necessary to compensate for the greater relative risk and added cost of setting up production facilities abroad. Typically, U. S. corporations have entered new and rapidly expanding industries like petro-chemicals, electronics, and machinery, while few investments were made in recent years in such traditional fields as steel or textiles. Yet by making new investments in these industries, new technology was transferred also, and the very dynamism that European industry enjoys today stems at least partly from this influx of new technology that is associated with U. S. investments in the newer industries. But let me postpone for the moment a full discussion of the technological impact of U. S. investments on Europe's industry.

Another aspect of the European concern about American corporations has to do with the comparatively great size—financial and otherwise—of the parent company in the United States. The notion exists that the vast resources of international companies might be used to crush smaller competitors through price-cutting or other predatory means. But past experience does not warrant this view. The large U. S. companies that have operated successfully in Europe have done so because they have been able to compete at lower prices with a better plant, a superior production process, or new products—in short, because of higher productivity or greater efficiency, and not because of financial power and unfair competition.

When studying this problem earlier this year one source, reporting on some of the findings of an EEC commission, noted that we can expect extensive industrial concentration in the Common Market in the course of the next several years, both because of technical progress and because of the new dimensions of the markets. In the course of this process, some corporations may well engage in intensive, even destructive, competition and others may be forced to merge or consolidate. In either event the danger of the appearance of "restrictive practices" and other antieconomic effects associated with the abuse of "dominant positions" is a real possibility. Nevertheless, the commission noted that such dangers will manifest themselves whether or not American firms participate in the process. It is true that American companies are technically better adapted to conditions of competition, and in many instances that they, through access to greater financial power, would be in a position to take greater advantage of their European competitors. As the commission noted, however, to prohibit or restrict access of American capital is not an effective solution to the problem of distorted conditions of competition.

In fact, such protection from foreign competition could very well stimulate the concentration process of European industry and lead to the same antieconomic consequences. In conclusion the commission reportedly observed that the solution to competitive abuses will not be found in restricting direct foreign investments, but rather in the development of effective regulations to maintain competition.

Another concern that is being voiced more frequently is related to the effects of U. S. investments on the balances of payments of the European nations. Direct investment affects the recipient country's balance of payments on at least three levels. The primary effect, of course, is the inflow of capital from the United States, and inasmuch as this flow is a drain on the U. S. balance of payments it benefits the recipient European country's payments balance. And although direct U. S. investments are relatively small in terms of the European economies, their impact on a nation's payments position is not insignificant. In 1962, for instance, net direct U. S. investment in Germany amounted to 250 million dollars, or a little over 2 percent of Germany's receipts from exports. But without this inflow, Germany's 1962 payments deficit would have been doubled and would have run to 500 million dollars. It is this latter point that has been stressed lately—that is, concern centers on the effects of a sharp reduction of the inflow of U. S. capital. Sometimes the point is made in Europe that U. S. investments will slow down and that this will produce a payments crisis. However, such forecasts seem rather unrealistic. For despite reports of declining profit margins in Europe, the inflow of direct U. S. investment capital has continued at a high level, and a recent McGraw-Hill survey shows that U. S. investment activity in Europe will continue at about the present rate in the years ahead, although an increasing portion of investment funds is expected to come from earnings generated in Europe. Piecing these facts together, it seems reasonable to suppose that the inflow of U. S. capital will not continue to grow. But neither is this flow likely to decline substantially unless some radical and unexpected change should occur in Europe.

The secondary effect of direct U. S. investments on Europe's payments position is the flow of dividends from European subsidiaries back to their parent companies in the United States. This return flow is, of course, an outflow from Europe's point of view and tends to offset the initial capital inflow. The general expectation is that the dividend flow back to the United States will grow in relation to the growth of U. S. investments in Europe and hence soon overtake the net outflow of capital. For example, private dividend flows to the United States from direct investments in Europe increased from a mere 270 million dollars in 1957 to 520 million dollars in 1962, and the Brookings Institution has estimated that such dividend payments from Europe may grow to 1,200 million dollars by 1968. By itself, any increased outflow will constitute a further drain on the various European payments balances. But I would like to mention two factors that may tend to ameliorate the impact of this effect.

One is the high proportion of earnings that are reinvested in Europe. As long as profits and sales opportunities are at least comparable or somewhat better in Europe than in the United States, a sizable share of U. S. subsidiary earnings will be reinvested rather than repatriated. And should European profit margins fall, dividend remittances could hardly increase. Thus, even though the flow of dividends back to the United States will increase, the size of this outflow is limited by both total earnings and opportunities for reinvestment. It will certainly not grow beyond a size that is easily within the ability of the European nations to adjust to.

The other factor that could possibly ameliorate the impact on the balance of payments of dividend payments by U. S. subsidiaries is a larger flow of dividend payments from U. S. parent companies to European stockholders. Already several large international companies have listed their stock on the European exchanges. An example is General Motors, where the following pattern of dividend flows may emerge. GM's British subsidiary remits part of its earnings as dividends to the United States-based parent company, which then returns these funds in the form of dividend payments by the parent company to British stockholders. True, such patterns of dividend flows are not very significant yet, but in future years a widespread and more international ownership of the large United States-based corporations may lead to a new attitude toward the large international or multinational corporation.

In addition to capital and dividend flows, many other effects on balances of payments can be traced to direct investment. For instance, a new United States-owned manufacturing facility may replace imports. It may also promote exports from Europe. On the other hand, U. S. subsidiaries often make payments of license and management fees to their respective parent companies; such payments totaled the sizable amount of 200 million dollars in 1962. Yet inasmuch as the total effect of direct U. S. investments in Europe on the U. S. balance of payments is largely neutral, the over-all effect on European payments balances is also neutral. Over the near future, the balance of payments flows may tip in favor of the United States, but the surplus we may generate on this account is at most rather small and, given healthy European trade balances, should not constitute a serious burden on European balances of payments.

So much for the balance of payments problem. I should like to turn now to a somewhat less controversial aspect of the U. S. corporation's activities in Europe—and one that I believe to be far more significant in the long run. I refer to the transfer of technological and managerial knowledge and to the establishment of business and personal links that have contributed to the economic development in Europe and to laying the groundwork for a stronger Atlantic Community.

Technological and Administrative Impact

The American corporations that have been investing and selling in Europe during the last ten years are drawn from the cream of the United States business community. Success in the competitive U. S. market is a natural prerequisite for investment in Europe, because only successful companies have both the means and the confidence to tackle the many problems of doing business abroad. And the successful domestic company also knows that business success in Europe depends on very much the same factors as business success in the United States.

Fundamentally, a direct investment involves so much more than transferring capital funds to Europe, which is actually the easiest part of the investment process. More important and more difficult is the actual building up and getting into operation of new manufacturing facilities, which involves the transfer and adaptation of technology and general business know-how—both essential for the ultimate success of a new business abroad. This process of bringing U. S. equipment, technology, management know-how, and highly trained personnel to bear on the European economy is, in my opinion, more significant than financial transactions because it affects and contributes to the basic economic strength of the European host country. For this reason, one must evaluate the impact of direct U. S. investments in Europe in terms of these real transfers as well.

Each new U. S. manufacturing facility established in Europe both expands industrial capacity and improves efficiency. Productive capacity is increased, because an additional amount of equipment has been put in place, contributing from then on to the host country's gross national output. Efficiency is improved, because American investments are typically in technologically advanced industries like electronics or chemicals, and in any event, involve production and management methods that are in some degree new to Europe and that are being used by U. S. subsidiaries and, later on perhaps, by European companies as well.

A crucial difference between American and European industry is that American industry allocates every year huge sums to industrial research and development, generally spending twice as much per dollar of sales on research and development as European companies do. Even more significant is the relative difference in the absolute amount of such expenditures, for surely technical and scientific advance depends on this latter measure, while expenditures per sales only indicate a company's awareness and willingness to invest in research and development programs. Here research and development spending by private U. S. industry averages at least five times greater than all of Europe's corresponding outlays. One reason why U. S. subsidiaries in Europe operate, on the average, more profitably than European companies is their access to the results of the U. S. parent companies' research and development programs. Because of this transfer of technology, Europe experienced a much faster postwar development in the new industries along the trail that had been blazed by U. S. companies in the American market.

There are various reasons why direct investment is the only certain way in which substantial amounts of technology are transferred. Most important is that licensing has some obvious limitations that tend to confine the amount and scope of technology passed along. The usual independent licensing agreement is confined to a specific process and too frequently does not create a relationship continuing beyond the first contract period, nor does it generally provide a strong foundation for technical flexibility. Further, compensation under licensing agreements is seldom deemed adequate to warrant the licensor's committing a great deal of time or energy to making such technical flexibility possible even if he were willing to do so. This generalization obviously does not apply to all patent licensing arrangements. On the other hand, it is clearly true that the broad-ranging technological transfer that takes place when American companies establish overseas operations has no substitute in the licensing area.

The knowledge that flows from the U. S. parent company to the subsidiary in Europe is, of course, not confined to technology but also includes various aspects of business administration. This science is well advanced in the United States, and every year American business schools train scores of future managers from foreign countries. However, we are all aware that an essential part of the science of business management is its day-to-day practice in a corporation. Again, this type of knowledge is being transferred only through direct investments when personnel and tested administrative procedures are employed in new subsidiaries in Europe. In time, such practices are absorbed by domestic companies. Simplifying administrative procedures and clarifying internal chains of authority are areas in which the example of U. S. subsidiaries may have stimulated the many apparent changes in European business life. As John Dunning has pointed out:

U. S. firms have also shown that it is not only technical efficiency which is an important determinant of the prosperity of a company, but that of the wider sphere of managerial control as well. It cannot be entirely coincidental that the industries in which American representation is most evidenced are also those which are both the most dynamic in character and which rely for their success on those variables which the U. S. economy is best suited to supply.[1]

Other areas in which improvements were initiated by U. S. companies are inventory management, equipment replacement policy, and, most important, management accounting and financial planning. And nobody can overlook Europe's postwar revolution in advertising and sales promotion that was kindled by American corporations and is sweeping the European business communities today.

The economic value of these changes must not be underestimated. Traditional practices—whether on the technical or administrative level—are difficult to change, and—as experience has shown—actual demonstration is usually required to do the trick of bringing about modernization. U. S. subsidiaries, operating in Europe and competing with domestic firms, have demonstrated many new techniques and practices that were then adopted by domestic companies. In my opinion, this process has contributed to the very substantial rates of annual productivity increases in Europe over the last decade.

[1] John H. Dunning, *American Investment in British Manufacturing Industry* (George Allen & Unwin, Ltd.), p. 189.

Social and Philosophical Impact

Closely related to the diffusion of U. S. technology and business practices is the slow but steady change that is taking place in European corporate philosophy. Most American corporations conceive their role to comprise a multitude of responsibilities—a responsibility to the stockholders of the corporation, to the employees of the company, to the public—the customers of the firm—to the nation at large, and to the corporate entity itself. From this broad-based conception of the corporation's role in modern society stems the public-mindedness of U. S. corporations and their relationship to the government. On the Continent, however, the idea of free enterprise had never been really accepted as a basic social value; rather, European business had always been involved in the shifting struggle of the social classes. This explains the relative secrecy of many European corporations, a practice that often shrouds the company's over-all performance. Recently, however, the annual reports of European corporations have become more informative and the need for a better corporate image is generally understood.

Related to this aspect of the impact that U. S. subsidiaries exert on the European business scene is the frequent criticism that United States-controlled companies often pay higher salaries than domestic firms and, therefore, tend to raise general salary levels. This specific charge is difficult to document, but it does focus on the often nontraditional hiring and promotion policies of American corporations in Europe. U. S. companies seem less bound to select management personnel according to the traditional European criteria of formal education and social standing, which are still widely used. Although the number of European managers employed in United States-controlled companies may not be large, the impact that U. S. companies have had in providing wider opportunities for talented management personnel has been significant. To this important extent, U. S. subsidiaries have contributed to an upgrading of Europe's management and a serious reevaluation of a system no longer able to cope with the realities of today.

To sum up this discussion, the impact of U. S. subsidiaries on European industry has been manifold and the European economies have received many benefits from it. But if this is indeed the case may we not conclude that U. S. subsidiaries as compared to local companies behave differently. The answer is Yes and No. U. S. subsidiaries differ from their European competitors to the extent that they introduce new methods of business operation and sales promotion, but they do not differ in terms of general business goals. Like any other company, the U. S. subsidiary in Europe aims at earning a good return on its investment by producing goods that can be sold profitably, that is, by manufacturing products that the public wants. Indeed, why should it matter whether biscuits sold in France are produced by French firms instead of by the local subsidiaries of American corporations? Regardless of ownership, either type of firm attempts to earn a good return and aims to expand sales. And both of these objectives can be accomplished by but one strategy only—to offer the best possible product at competitive prices. This simple maxim of business behavior holds true for automobiles, office machines, petro-chemicals, electrical equipment, as well as for biscuits.

Needless to say, within any European country a U. S. subsidiary is subject to the same laws and taxes as domestic companies. This is at it should be and the few special regulations that exist in some countries are really specific forms of investment incentives. By and large, however, European domestic companies and U. S. subsidiaries operate under the same conditions and have the same general business goals.

I think it should be pointed out here that the entry of American corporations into the European markets is a very different development from the investment activity and investment philosophy that marked colonialism in previous centuries. Many such investments simply used a colony's resources without accumulating capital, without expanding productive capacity within the country, without training and employing native labor in management jobs, and without contributing to the host country's general economic development.

Clearly, present-day international business is an entirely different specie than the colonial-type investment. The large, multinational companies of the present age regard the major regional markets of the world as complementary markets in which to do business on a permanent basis. This is emphasized by the fact that in the last eight years American corporations have reinvested a higher proportion of their European earnings in Europe than they have in the United States—a very far cry indeed from nineteenth-century exploitation.

Of course, in order to be successful in the various markets of the world, the large international companies—whether American or European—cannot afford to base all their decisions on any one nation's economic policy. Instead, they must attempt to balance their world-wide operations by taking into account political and economic conditions around the world. The opportunity to shift production and sales from one market to another gives the international corporation an element of freedom that purely local firms do not have. It also means that multinational firms become less dependent on any one nation's trade policies, particularly tariffs and import quotas.

There are some governments that fear the greater freedom of international companies that comes from the broadening of their field of action. The feeling on the part of these governments is that an international company's decisions on where to produce how much do not take account of the local social and political environment and may, therefore, not serve the best interests of the community. To take a specific example, assume that a European plant of a U. S. corporation has been either losing money or making less than other subsidiaries of the corporation. When management finally decides to move or close down the plant, the result may be local unemployment, lower tax revenues, and so forth. The importance of these social burdens is in no way to be slighted, of course, but the remedy is clearly not to order a company to keep operating at a loss.

In any event, shutdowns of plants are relatively rare, and given the premise that companies want to show a profit, shutdowns or locational moves are unlikely to be done capriciously. Indeed, their causes invariably are underlying economic conditions, and the only difference in the reaction of local and subsidiary operations is that international corporations may react more quickly to an untenable situation.

From another point of view, however, the emergence of international companies investing freely on both sides of the Atlantic is truly a welcome development. In the not so distant future, I can see a structure of the world market in which the large and dynamic manufacturing companies have production facilities all over the globe and in which the major firms compete in the regional markets through local subsidiaries. Such a world structure of industry will put the larger companies on an equal footing within each area—a goal that has been the strongest single incentive to invest abroad since World War II. The present entry of American corporations into the European market is only the beginning in the general development toward a world industry.

Direct investment by corporate firms seems best suited for the rapid and meaningful diffusion of capital and technological know-how—in short, of industrial wealth. It also has the effect of intertwining the various national economies in a more complete sense than a free trade area can hope to accomplish. Thus, direct U. S. investment in Western Europe is much more than building a warehouse or acquiring a local company. Its long-range effect of creating a vast community of common business interests provides the real underpinnings for an Atlantic community. And because, to my mind, the forming of a multitude of links across the Atlantic is a very good thing,

I wish to conclude by saying that I am very much in favor of international investments. It is good business and it is good politics. The more American companies there are in Europe and the more European companies there are in the United States, the larger is our range of common interests and the greater our mutual understanding, our cooperation, and our friendship.

The links that are being forged today between Europe and the United States are no longer just at the governmental level but have penetrated the surface of official relations and are increasingly improved by a broadening base of mutual economic interests. Governments are finding it more difficult to turn inward to isolationism, and internationalism is increasingly becoming a fact of life. I am happy to say that U. S. business is playing an important role in helping to bring this about.

3.

THE EUROPEAN COMMON MARKET IN

ECONOMIC PERSPECTIVE

Howard S. Piquet
Senior Specialist in International Economics
Legislative Reference Service
The Library of Congress

Introduction

It is important that the facts and probabilities with regard to trade relations between the U. S. and the European Economic Community be placed in perspective, lest policies be adopted that might harm the long-run interests of the United States and the Free World generally. To do this it is necessary that (1) figures with respect to trade and economic growth be understood; (2) these figures be interpreted in the light of what economic history teaches regarding relationships between industrialization and trade; (3) the economics of the EEC be examined in light of the international financial problems of the West, and (4) the attitudes of all the leaders of the EEC be given proper weight. A strong leader can influence history, but he is not its long-run determinant—not even President de Gaulle.

Were it not for strong *political* motivation, integration of the economies of the six countries comprising the European Economic Community would not have been undertaken, and, without continued political motivation, the goal of European economic unity will not be reached. The drive toward integration in Western Europe is so great that even the obstacles that have been created by the intransigence of President de Gaulle will not keep it from materializing—eventually.

Although the idea of a united Europe is not new, it remained a dream until World War II convinced European leaders of the inadequacies and dangers inherent in a system of completely sovereign, relatively small, national States. All six countries comprising the Community suffered military defeat in World War II, all six went through periods of occupation by foreign military powers, and all six suffered tremendous human and material losses. Meanwhile, the United States was expanding its economy, while the Soviet Union and the forces of international communism were becoming increasingly threatening. It became clear that, to retain their independence, Europeans would have to abandon traditional national jealousies and work together to expand markets and attain widespread prosperity. The Marshall Plan gave the initial impetus, but it was not long before Western Europe was forging ahead under its own power.

Background

The United States has supported consistently the principle of European integration because it is convinced that the existence of a broad, competitive market in Western Europe will enhance the strength of the Free World and in the long run be in its own interest. In 1947–1948, in inaugurating the Marshall Plan for economic aid to Europe, the United States urged that the recipient countries cooperate among themselves, economically and politically, and many times has reaffirmed its interest in a unified Europe.

Formation of the seventeen-country Organization for European Economic Cooperation (OEEC) was a direct result of this suggestion. Its immediate purpose was to allocate aid received under the Marshall Plan, but the urgency of the common problems of Western Europe was so great that it soon came to serve larger purposes, principally as an instrument for reducing import quotas and for facilitating international payments among the member countries. Useful though it has been, the OEEC—as well as its successor, the Organization for Economic Cooperation and Development, which includes the United States and Canada together with the original members of the former OEEC—is little more than an international committee that does not provide the economic unity which progressive leaders of Europe feel is necessary.

By 1950 Western Europe was well along the road to economic recovery, and its most important political problem was how to defend itself against the military threat of the Soviet Union. Belgium and Luxembourg, which had created their customs union in 1921, had agreed with the Netherlands during World War II to expand the union to include all three countries. Soon after the war this was accomplished in the form of Benelux.

In 1952 these three countries, together with France, Italy, and West Germany established a common market for coal and steel, and since then tariffs and quotas on these products among the six countries have been abolished. The formation of the Coal and Steel Community was of great significance because, for the first time, important supranational supervisory institutions were created. Its significance was heightened when it provided the framework for the broader European Economic Community.

In 1954 an unsuccessful attempt was made to form a European Defense Community, together with a companion political community. The failure did not halt the drive for Western European unity, however, and the movement was revived by the formation of Euratom and the EEC, which became effective in 1958. The drive toward European unity is strong because it responds to deep-seated political desires, principal among which are the urges to (1) end the historic animosity between France and Germany, (2) substitute a strong European entity for the individual European nation-states, and (3) create a European entity large enough to negotiate with the United States and the Soviet Union on the principle that common European interests are more important than narrower, national interests.

The European Common Market Is Created

The European Economic Community, created by the Treaty of Rome (1957) is the most ambitious step yet taken toward economic integration in Western Europe. The most important aspect of the Community, from the point of view of the United States economy, is the European Common Market, under which the six member countries agreed to eliminate all tariffs and quotas among themselves, starting January 1, 1959. It was contemplated that twelve to fifteen years would be required for the progressive attainment of free trade within the area, but the member countries soon agreed to speed up the timetable and, by July 1, 1963, internal tariffs had been reduced to 40 percent of their 1957 levels for industrial products and to 60 percent for agricultural items. The target date for the complete elimination of internal tariffs is now January 1, 1967, instead of 1969–1972, as originally planned.

The European Common Market, which is a customs union, differs from a free trade area in that it not only provides for free trade among its member countries but it also establishes a common external tariff against imports from countries that are not members of the Community. Under the Treaty of Rome the common external tariff rates that are applicable to goods imported from nonmember countries are to be uniform, and most of them are to be determined by the arithmetic averages of the tariffs of the individual member countries. The final common external tariff was to be arrived at in three stages—30 percent toward the ultimate level by December 31, 1961; another 30 percent by December 31, 1965; and the final 40 percent by December 31, 1969. However, the first 30 percent adjustments were made on December 31, 1960, a full year ahead of the original timetable. With respect to industrial products, another 30 percent reduction in the difference between the national tariffs and the common external tariff became effective on July 1, 1963.

For a large number of products the EEC countries are

granting temporary concessions to the contracting parties to the General Agreement on Tariffs and Trade (GATT). The latest 30 percent adjustment, referred to above, applies to the difference between the national tariffs of each of the member countries and the common external tariff, reduced by 20 percent. The EEC has announced that continuance of this concession will depend upon the results of the tariff negotiations to be held under the auspices of the GATT in 1964.

Because of the acceleration of internal tariff reduction and the early institution of the common external tariff, the impact of the external common tariff of the EEC on United States exports is being felt somewhat earlier than had been anticipated. Since the common external tariff is to be determined by the average of rates in each of the six countries in 1957, the tariffs that eventually will be applicable to U. S. products exported to certain member countries will be higher than before, while those applicable to exports to other member countries will be lower. Generally speaking, the tariffs of France and Italy will be lower, whereas those of Benelux and West Germany will be higher.

Although the common external tariff is to be arrived at by averaging the tariffs of the individual member countries, it is not necessary, where reductions in existing tariffs are called for, that each and every tariff rate be reduced equally. The treaty allows members, in reducing tariffs to arrive at the common average, to reduce those on weak industries more slowly than the average. The annexes to the treaty contain seven special lists of commodities that are to be dutiable under the common external tariff at rates not in excess of specified maximums. One list (List F) includes eighty-seven products on which the common tariff is to be fixed by mutual agreement. The most important list (List G) names commodities on which the common tariff rates are left to future negotiation among the member countries. There are about seventy items on this list, some of which are important to American exporters, including lard, certain animal and vegetable oils, lead and zinc ores, sulphur, engines for motor vehicles, certain machine tools, and transmission gear for motor vehicle engines.

The results of future negotiations with nonmember countries regarding these tariffs will be an indication of the long-run attitude of the EEC toward nonmember countries. It is not yet known whether the Community will be outward-looking, in line with the intentions of the founding fathers of Western European unity (including Jean Monnet and Walter Hallstein), or whether it will be inward-looking, in line with the philosophy of President de Gaulle. Much will depend upon the willingness of nonmember countries to negotiate with the EEC for the elimination of external trade barriers.

Import quotas are to be eliminated within the Common Market by the end of the transition period. Although the Treaty of Rome does not specifically cover quotas on imports from nonmember countries, its preamble expresses a desire to contribute to the general removal of restrictions on international trade.

Agricultural policy has presented some of the knottiest problems that the European Economic Community has had to face. After long and difficult negotiations, general agreement was reached in January 1962, and first steps were taken toward establishing a common agricultural policy. Broad decisions were made affecting wheat, flour, feed grains, poultry and eggs, pork, fruits, vegetables, and wine. At the same time, the end of 1969 was set as the target date for completion of the common market for agricultural products. By then, all tariffs, quotas, and other regulations restricting intracommunity trade in agricultural products are to be removed and national agricultural policies harmonized. At that time also, all individual-country tariffs are to be replaced by a uniform system of tariffs for the Community as a whole.

For some commodities variable levies are to apply. These are tariffs that are intended to equal the difference between world prices and desired price objectives within the Common Market. Such a system can promote self-sufficiency and, by providing strong price incentives for the expansion of production within the EEC area, together with protection against import competition, can result in an expansion of uneconomic production. As far as the United States is concerned, feed grains and wheat are the most important products that will be affected.

Other Important Features of the EEC

The European Economic Community is more than a customs union. It is an *economic* union, in that it looks toward the ultimate merging of the economies of the six member countries. The essential characteristic of such a union is that the factors of production—labor, capital, and enterprise—are to be allowed to move freely among the member countries. The treaty specifically provides that the principle of equal wages for men and women, for equal work, is to prevail.

The member countries are also to undertake to improve and harmonize living conditions within the Community and to commit themselves to coordinate monetary and fiscal policies for the purpose of promoting balance in international payments, high employment, and price stability. The treaty provides for a European Investment Bank and a Development Fund for associated overseas territories for the purpose of transferring capital to the less developed parts of the Community and to the associated areas. The treaty also establishes a Social Fund designed to improve employment possibilities of labor within the Community. Its principal purpose is to finance the retraining and resettlement of workers who may be injured by liberalization of trade within the Community.

The Rome Treaty is particularly significant in that it establishes institutions that are not subordinate to any national government. Like its predecessor, the Coal and Steel Community, the EEC is *supra*national, rather than *inter*national in character. The institutions of the EEC are a Commission, a Council of Ministers, an Assembly, and a Court of Justice. The Assembly and the Court serve Euratom and the Coal and Steel Community as well as the EEC. Even though the treaty does not make political union an explicit objective, many Europeans believe that the Treaty of Rome is an important step in the evolution of a United States of Europe.

The European Free Trade Association (EFTA)

The United Kingdom and a number of other European countries, favoring freer trade but believing that European economic integration should follow a loose cooperative pattern rather than the supranational approach of the EEC and the Coal and Steel Community, proposed the creation of an inclusive European Free Trade Area, embracing all members of the OEEC. Under this proposal, the member countries would agree to eliminate tariffs among themselves over a period of years. Objections on the part of the United Kingdom to the supranational, customs-union approach were understandable in view of the system of preferential tariffs underlying trade among the British Commonwealth countries.

Nothing concrete materialized from the proposal, however, and in January 1959 the first internal tariff cuts were made by the EEC on schedule. Several months later delegates from the United Kingdom, Norway, Sweden, Denmark, Switzerland, Austria, and Portugal formed their own free trade area. They signed the Stockholm Convention establishing the European Free Trade Association (EFTA) and agreed to abolish all tariffs among themselves on industrial goods. Special arrangements were made to stimulate trade in agricultural and fishery products. Tariffs against each other were to be reduced by 20 percent on July 1, 1960, and by further annual cuts of 10 percent until January 1970, at which time all tariffs among the seven countries would be eliminated.

As in the case of the EEC, elimination of protective tariffs among the member countries of the EFTA will be discriminatory against imports from the United States and other countries outside the organization. The schedule of tariff reductions called for by the Stockholm Convention was accelerated so as to bring tariffs among the seven member countries down to 70 percent of their former level on July 1, 1961—six months ahead of schedule. By January 1, 1963 they had been reduced to 50 percent of their original levels, and in May 1963, the EFTA Council announced that the timetable for the elimination of the final 50 percent would be by 10-percent stages on December 31 of each year until December 31, 1966, at which time they would be eliminated completely.

Because EFTA does not establish a common external tariff, its members had to devise rules to prevent goods from being shipped into a low-tariff country for distribution throughout EFTA at reduced rates of duty. Each member maintains its own external tariff.

The United Kingdom and the EEC

After it became clear that the European Free Trade Association could not forestall its establishment, the United Kingdom decided to join the European Economic Community. Formal application for membership was made in August 1961, following an overwhelmingly favorable vote in the House of Commons. Denmark and Ireland soon applied for membership also.

The United Kingdom made this move, nothwithstanding the difficulties that she faced in her relations with other British Commonwealth countries and the near-impossibility of reconciling her agricultural policies with those of Continental Europe.

Britain's application for membership met stiff opposition from President de Gaulle, and, after many conferences and much bitterness, just as it seemed that agreement was about to be reached, the EEC denied the application. Because of the outspoken desire of the United States that Britain join the EEC, there has been widespread feeling that de Gaulle's slap at the British really was intended to be a slap at the United States, since he has been consistently opposed to expanding American influence in Europe.

For the immediate future, at least, the question of British membership in the EEC is closed. This is not to say that the door to membership will not some day be reopened, however. If and when the United Kingdom does tie its economy to that of Continental Europe, the way will be opened for wider trans-Atlantic cooperation, which continues to be an important objective of United States foreign policy.

Had the British application for membership in the EEC been accepted, the complexion of the European Economic Community would be substantially different from that which seems to be evolving. It is because of antagonism to "outside" influences that President de Gaulle has been opposed to an economic bridge across the English Channel, and thence to the United States.

This antagonism is the external aspect of his continued appeal for a "partnership of Fatherlands" in Continental Europe.

Now that the question of British membership in the EEC has been temporarily settled, it becomes necessary for the United States and Great Britain, and other countries outside the EEC, to decide what, if anything, they should do to bring about closer partnership among themselves, with or without cooperation of the EEC. Thinking along these lines has been fogged by confusion between membership in the Community and trade relations with it. It is not necessary to be a member of the Community to trade with it or to negotiate with it for the reduction of trade barriers. The door is still open to expand trade among the countries of the Free World, including the EEC.

The EEC and the United States Compared

There has been little disagreement in the United States regarding the desirability of the political integration of Western Europe. Most Americans are aware that the United States has a deep interest in the success of the EEC in bringing about political solidarity among its member countries, while maintaining harmonious relations with other European countries. There has been general agreement, ever since the days of the Marshall Plan, that the United States interest is best served by a Europe that is united and strong.

In a general way, also, Americans are aware of the desirability of European economic integration and development, hoping it will proceed in such a way as to advance the economic well-being of the entire Free World.

However, feeling has not been unanimous regarding the probable effects of the Common Market on United States foreign trade. That the gradual abolition of tariffs among the member countries themselves and the establishment of a common external tariff will discriminate to an increasing degree against imports from the United States and other countries outside the Community is evident. But opinions differ as to whether such discrimination constitutes a long-term, as well as a short-term, threat to U. S. exports. Some believe it is, while others believe that the short-term discrimination is relatively unimportant compared with the long-run, beneficial economic effects of a strong and rapidly growing Western Europe.

As is usually the case in such circumstances, arguments range all the way from apparently objective factual presentations to alarmist expressions of fear. It is stated, for example, that the EEC countries have been experiencing a rate of economic growth which is much more rapid than that of the United States and that, unless the rate of growth of the United States economy is increased substantially, the United States is headed for economic disaster. The facts are as stated, but they do not necessarily lead to such a conclusion.

Neither complacency nor fear is justified by the available facts. It is necessary that the statistics be interpreted objectively and in the light of history and economic principles.

The Economy of the EEC

The six countries comprising the European Economic Community have a population only slightly smaller than that of the United States. Although their combined gross national product in 1961 was only 201 billion dollars, compared with 518 billion dollars for the United States, their total external trade (total exports and imports, excluding trade among themselves) was over 20 percent larger than the total foreign trade of the United States. On a per capita basis, the gross national product of the EEC was 1,178 dollars, compared with 2,820 dollars for the United States (Table 1).

Rates of Economic Growth

Comparisons of rates of economic growth, even when the entities being compared are homogeneous enough to be subjected to mathematical measurement, can lead to erroneous conclusions unless they are interpreted in relation to the absolute magnitudes to which they refer.

The economy of the European Economic Community is growing and gives promise of continuing to grow steadily, but the fact that its gross national product has been expanding at 5½ percent per annum compared with 2½ percent for the United States (at constant prices) does not mean that it will continue to grow at that rate after its economy doubles, or triples, in size, thereby approaching the magnitude of the gross national product of the United States.

TABLE 1
Economies of the United States, the
European Economic Community, and the United
Kingdom, 1961

	Population	Gross National Product		External Trade[1]	
		Total (billions)	Per Capita	Exports (billions)	Imports (billions)
United States	183,742,000	$518.2	$2,820	$20.6	$14.4
EEC	170,603,000	201.0	1,178	20.6[1]	20.7[1]
United Kingdom	53,441,000	75.0	1,403	10.7	12.3
[Estimated world total]				[122.2]	

[1] Not including trade between the EEC countries themselves. Intra-EEC trade: 11.8 billion dollars.

Notwithstanding an increase of 54 per cent in the gross national product of the EEC between 1953 and 1961, compared with an increase of only 21 percent in that of the United States (Table 2), the smaller rate of increase for the United States represented an expansion of 79 billion dollars compared with an expansion of only 58 billion dollars for the EEC.

The important thing is not the game of mathematical musical chairs. Rather, it is the obvious observation that if the rates of growth of the EEC and the United States remain at their 1953–1961 levels (5½ percent and 2½ percent, respectively) the economy of the EEC will be over half the size of the U. S. economy by 1973. In that event, the volume of the gross national product of both the EEC and the U. S. will have increased by approximately 180 billion dollars.

Per-capita Comparisons

The picture is brought into clearer focus if comparisons are made over a longer period of time, on a per-capita basis and in terms of dollars of constant purchasing power. On this basis, the combined per-capita gross national product of the EEC countries increased 43 percent between 1953 and 1961, compared with an increase of approximately 6 per cent in that of the United States. However, if comparisons are made for the twenty-two-year period starting just prior to the outbreak of World War II (1938) the per-capita gross national product of the EEC is seen to have expanded more slowly than that of the United States between 1938 and 1960.

As shown in Tables 2 and 3, the United States experienced its most rapid per-capita growth between 1938 and 1953. Since 1953 the western European countries have been catching up. Until 1950 Western Europe was recovering from the war with substantial assistance from the United States under the Marshall Plan. Since then it has been growing rapidly without outside assistance. Between 1953 and 1961 its aggregate GNP expanded at an

TABLE 2

Gross National Products, in Constant (1954)[1] Prices: EEC and United States (1953-1961) (In U. S. Dollars)

Year	EEC (billions)	U. S. (billions)	Per Capita[2]	
			EEC	U. S.
1953	$106.6	$370.7	$671	$2,312
1954	112.8	364.8	704	2,237
1955	121.6	394.0	753	2,375
1956	128.1	401.5	787	2,377
1957	134.9	409.8	821	2,384
1958	138.2	403.3	832	2,307
1959	145.2	430.1	866	2,419
1960	155.9	441.2	922	2,442
1961	164.1	449.4	960	2,446
Increase (1953-1961)	+53.9%	+21.2%	+43.1%	+5.8%
Annual Average	+5½ %	+2½ %	+4½ %	¾ of 1%

[1] In 1954 prices and 1958 exchange rates.
[2] Population: EEC—158.9 million in 1953; 170.9 million in 1961.
       U. S.—160.3 million in 1953; 183.7 million in 1961.
SOURCE: OECD Statistical Bulletins.

TABLE 3
Per-Capita Gross National Products,
in Constant Purchasing Power, 1938,
1953, 1960 [1]
(In U. S. Dollars)

Year	EEC	U. S.	U. K.
1938	$601	$1,303	$ 720
1953	715	2,314	940
1960	976	2,458	1,113
Percentage Changes			
1938–1953	+19.0	+77.6	+30.6
1953–1960	+36.5	+ 6.2	+18.4
1938–1960	+62.4	+88.6	+54.6

[1] In 1954 prices and 1954 exchange rates.
SOURCE: Derived from OECD Statistical Bulletins. Figures for 1938 based on "Trends in Economic Growth," Legislative Reference Service, Library of Congress (Washington, D. C.: Government Printing Office, 1955), p. 269.

annual average rate of 5½ percent, compared with an annual average rate for the United States of 2½ percent. Because the population of the United States has been increasing much more rapidly than that of the EEC countries combined, the relative rates of increase on a percapita basis, in terms of constant prices, have been 4½ percent for the EEC countries and ¾ of 1 percent for the United States.

It would be erroneous to conclude that the average European is economically better off than the average American simply because the rate of growth of the European economy has been more rapid than that of the

United States. In 1961 the per-capita GNP of the United States was 2,820 dollars, while that of the EEC was 1,178 dollars.[1] Purely as an exercise in arithmetic, with the GNP of the United States growing at 3 percent, and that of the EEC at 5½ percent, per annum, and on the assumption that the spread between per-capita rates of increase in GNP will continue, it will require over a quarter of a century for the EEC to catch up with the United States.

The formation of the European Common Market was feasible largely because of the steady economic progress of Western Europe after 1950. Now that the EEC promises to become an accomplished fact, the economic expansion of the member countries ought to be substantial and steady. In all probability, the big growth of the Community lies in the future.

[1] Gross national product figures show the estimated value of all goods and services produced. Recent studies of consumer expenditures, which provide a better measure of current economic abundance for the population as a whole than the gross national product, indicate approximately the same per-capita ratios between the EEC and the United States (1:2.5). In 1961, per-capita consumer expenditures in the EEC totaled 719 dollars, while in the United States they totaled 1,805 dollars. These figures are computed on the basis of current foreign exchange rates, which tend to understate the purchasing power of consumer incomes in Europe, compared with those in the United States. It has been estimated that, on the basis of "purchasing power" exchange rates —the relative internal purchasing power of money—per-capita consumer expenditures in the EEC in 1961 totaled 964 dollars, compared with 1,805 dollars in the United States. On this basis, per-capita consuming power in the EEC was approximately 53 percent as large as in the United States (compared with 40 percent, on the basis of monetary exchange rates).

External Trade of the Common Market

Almost 40 percent of the total foreign trade of the countries comprising the Common Market consists of trade among the member countries themselves. This trade will become "internal" trade after the Common Market is fully established. Trade with nonmember countries, which will then be "external" trade, amounted to approximately 43 billion dollars in 1962, about evenly divided between exports and imports.

Forty-five percent of the external exports of the EEC go to nonmember countries in Europe, and about 12 percent to the United States (2.4 billion dollars in 1962). On the import side, nonmember countries in Europe supply about 30 percent of the EEC's total external imports, and the United States, about 16 percent (3.6 billion dollars in 1962). The United States is about 50 percent more important to the EEC as a source of imports than it is as a market for the Community's exports (Table 4).

Imports into the EEC countries from nonmember countries, as is to be expected, have been increasing more slowly than trade among the member countries themselves. Between 1958 and 1962 total imports into the EEC countries increased 71 percent. Imports from member countries increased 94 percent, while imports from nonmember countries increased 59 percent. Imports from the United States, however, increased only 48 percent, compared with an increase in imports from other nonmember countries of 78 percent (Table 5). Imports into the EEC countries from nonmember countries have been

TABLE 4
External Trade of the EEC, 1962
(In millions)

	Exports	Percentage Distribution	Imports	Percentage Distribution
TOTAL TRADE	$34,248	—	$35,717	—
Intra-EEC trade	13,395	—	13,395	—
EXTERNAL TRADE	20,853	100.0 [60.9]	22,322	100.0 [62.5]
EFTA	7,500	36.0	5,508	24.7 15.4
Other Europe	1,872	9.0 21.9	1,268	5.7 3.6
U. S.	2,448	11.7 5.5	3,630	16.3 10.2
Canada	312	1.5 7.1	452	2.0 1.3
Latin America	1,872	9.0 0.9	2,312	10.4 6.5
Japan	309	1.5 5.5	257	1.1 0.7
Other	6,540	31.4 0.9 19.1	8,895	39.8 24.8

SOURCE: Statistical Bulletins of the OECD.

TABLE 5
Trends in Foreign Trade of the EEC, 1958–1962
(In billions)

	1958	1960	1962	Percentage Change 1958–1962
TOTAL IMPORTS	$20.9	$29.6	$35.7	+71
Intra-EEC	6.9	10.1	13.4	+94
Nonmembers	14.0	19.5	22.3	+59
U. S.	2.4	3.5	3.6	+48
Other nonmembers	10.5	16.0	18.7	+78
TOTAL EXPORTS	$22.8	$29.7	$34.2	+50
Intra-EEC	6.9	10.1	13.4	+94
Nonmembers	15.9	19.6	20.8	+31
U. S.	1.7	2.3	2.4	+45
Other nonmembers	14.2	17.3	18.4	+30

maintaining a fairly constant ratio of approximately 10 percent of the area's combined gross national product (constant prices, at 1958 exchange rates).

During the same period, total exports of the EEC countries increased 50 percent. Exports to nonmember countries increased only 31 percent, compared with a 94-percent increase in intra-EEC exports. Exports to the United States increased more rapidly than exports to other nonmember countries—by 45 percent and 30 percent, respectively.

Importance of Western Europe in U. S. Foreign Trade

The foreign trade of the United States increased 6.7 billion dollars between 1958 and 1962—exports by 3.6 billion dollars, and imports by 3.1 billion dollars. Over 50 percent of the increased exports, and almost 39 percent of the increased imports, were accounted for by trade with Western Europe, as the following tabulation shows.

The net increase in the total volume of foreign trade of the United States with Western Europe during this period was larger than the increase with any other area, totaling 3.1 billion dollars. It was approached only by increased trade with the Far East, which totaled 2.8 billion dollars. Over 60 percent of the increase in the volume of trade with Western Europe was accounted for by trade with the six EEC countries. Western Europe is the most impor-

Net Increases in Total Volume of U. S. Trade, 1958–1962
(In billions)

	Exports	Imports	Exports and Imports
TOTAL	$3.6	$3.1	$6.7
Western Europe	1.9	1.2	3.1
[EEC]	[1.2]	[0.7]	[1.9]
Far East	1.6	1.2	2.8
All other (Net)	0.1	0.7	0.8

tant market for U. S. exports, as well as the largest source of U. S. imports. In 1962 exports to the area amounted to 6.4 billion dollars and accounted for almost one-third of total U. S. exports. Imports from Western Europe totaled 4.5 billion dollars and accounted for over 27 percent of total imports (Table 6).

The six EEC countries together accounted for 18.5 percent of all U.S. exports, and for approximately 15 percent of all U.S. imports. As a market for U.S. exports, the EEC is almost as important as Canada. It is considerably less important than Canada, however, as a source of imports, notwithstanding the fact that imports from the EEC have been increasing much more rapidly than imports from Canada. Although U.S. exports to, and imports from, the EEC countries have been increasing at about the same rate since 1958 (over 45 percent), exports still exceed imports by 1.2 billion dollars.

Exports to the seven EFTA countries, which have been increasing more rapidly than imports from them, are still several hundred million dollars larger than imports.

How Will the Common Market Affect the United States?

One is tempted to project the factors affecting U.S. exports to the EEC countries in order to arrive at conclusions regarding the probable effects of the Common Market upon the U.S. economy. Such projections can be dangerous, particularly if they are conceived of as forecasts, because for every mathematically measurable vari-

TABLE 6
U. S. Exports and Imports by Region, 1958–1962
(In billions)

EXPORTS [1]

	1958	1960	1961	1962	Percentage Distribution 1962	Percentage Change 1958–1962
TOTAL	$15.9	$18.9	$19.1	$19.5	100.0	+22.3
Canada	3.4	3.7	3.6	3.8	19.5	+11.4
American Republics	4.1	3.5	3.4	3.2	16.4	−7.5
Western Europe	4.5	6.3	6.3	6.4	32.8	+41.1
EEC	[2.4]	[3.5]	[3.5]	[3.6]	[18.5]	+48.2
EFTA	[1.4]	[2.3]	[2.0]	[2.0]	[10.3]	+35.3
Other	[0.7]	[0.5]	[0.8]	[0.8]	[4.0]	+14.3
Japan	0.8	1.3	1.7	1.4	7.2	+67.3
Other Far East	1.6	2.3	2.3	2.6	13.3	+59.8
All other	1.5	1.8	1.8	2.1	10.8	+40.0

IMPORTS [2]

	1958	1960	1961	1962	Percentage Distribution 1962	Percentage Change 1958–1962
TOTAL	$13.3	$15.0	$14.7	$16.4	100.0	+23.7
Canada	3.0	3.1	3.3	3.7	22.6	+23.3
American Republics	3.6	3.5	3.2	3.4	20.7	−5.4
Western Europe	3.3	4.2	4.1	4.5	27.4	+37.8
EEC	[1.7]	[2.3]	[2.2]	[2.4]	[14.6]	+45.6
EFTA	[1.4]	[1.6]	[1.5]	[1.7]	[10.4]	+25.6
Other	[0.2]	[0.3]	[0.4]	[0.4]	[2.4]	+50.0
Japan	0.7	1.1	1.1	1.4	8.5	+102.4
Other Far East	1.2	1.5	1.5	1.7	10.4	+31.1
All other	1.5	1.6	1.5	1.7	10.4	+13.3

[1] Including reexports; excluding special category exports.
[2] General imports.

SOURCE: U. S. Department of Commerce.

able there are scores of others that, though known to exist, cannot be measured, together with hundreds of others that are not even recognizable.

Among the factors that can be measured, at least in a rough way, are the gross national products of the EEC countries (the estimated total value of all goods and services produced), recent rates of increase in these GNP's, ratios of imports to gross national products, and the U.S. share of EEC imports. These are aggregates that can be estimated and projected into the future. There are, however, many others that cannot be measured, but that are of vital importance in determining the aggregate volume and composition of trade—among them, changed individual price relationships resulting from changes in conditions of supply and demand, research and development, and consequent technological changes. These variables are as incommensurate as attitudes toward tariffs and other trade restrictions and other political factors.

Businessmen and the public generally are disposed to be more concerned over the short-run than the long-run outlook, notwithstanding that the latter may often be more important, even to them as individuals, than the former. In the long run the importance of the European Common Market to the United States involves such concepts as the gross volume of trade (regardless, for the most part, of its composition) and the per-capita incomes of the people. Herein lies the difference between the national point of view and the points of view of individuals who, being engaged in particular lines of production or trade, think primarily in terms of the sales outlook this season and the next.

Mathematical projections are more significant in the short run than in the long run. Rates of economic growth, ratios of imports to gross national products, and other observable relationships are not likely to change very much over short periods of time. Over longer time periods, however, they change radically. The longer the time period the less important the currently observable relationships are and the more important it is that judgments be based on historical experience and economic theory.

One's appraisal of the likely effects of the Common Market upon U.S. exports is likely to be pessimistic, or optimistic, depending upon the observer's time period. The shorter it is the more alarming the outlook seems to be. Conversely, the longer the time period, the more optimistic it appears to be. Most serious attempts to appraise the probable effects of the Common Market upon the U.S. economy have been from the short-run point of view, that is, attempts to appraise what is likely to happen within the next three to five years.[2]

Short-run Effects on U. S. Exports

Over relatively short spans of years there tends to be a fairly constant relationship between a country's gross national product and its imports. External imports of the EEC (imports from nonmember countries) in recent

[2] The most elaborate short-run projections that have been published are those contained in a recent report of The Brookings Institution, "The United States Balance of Payments in 1968," which was prepared at the request of the Council of Economic Advisers (Washington, D. C.: U. S. Government Printing Office, August 1963).

years have averaged about 10 percent of their combined gross national product, of which imports supplied by the United States have accounted for 17 percent.

In terms of constant prices (1954 base) the average per annum rate of growth of the six EEC countries has been 5½ percent.

If these percentages are applied to the figures for 1961 on a simple, straight-line basis, the GNP of the EEC would increase from 201 billion dollars to 292 billion in 1968, and external imports would increase from 20.4 to 29.2 billion dollars (Table 7). On the assumption that the United States continues to supply the same proportion of the EEC's total external imports, the share supplied by the U.S. would increase from 3.5 billion dollars to 5.0 billion in 1968. This increase of 5 billion dollars may be considered as the growth potential of U.S. exports to the EEC, on the basis of the assumptions stated, were it not for the tariff discrimination against imports from non-member countries that is being introduced by the freeing of trade within the EEC and the imposition of a common external tariff.

Manufactured goods are predominant in U.S. exports to the EEC, as well as in imports from the area. U.S. exports to the EEC, in 1961, by broad commodity classifications, were as follows:

	Millions	Percentage Distribution
Manufactured goods	$1,644	47
Agricultural products	1,188	35
Nonagricultural raw materials	673	18
TOTAL	$3,505	100

Discrimination against manufactured goods will be particularly severe in certain lines. American producers will find it difficult, for example, to sell certain kinds of machinery and chemicals in the Common Market in competition with low-cost German producers. German manufacturers will find it easier than before to sell in other EEC countries because internal tariffs will be eliminated. At the same time, American manufacturers will have to pay the common external tariff to sell anywhere in the Common Market. In many cases the new tariff will be higher than it was prior to the formation of the EEC.

Comparisons of the competitive effects of tariffs are obscured by the fact that statistical classifications of manufactured goods are too broad to be indicative of the incidence of the tariff on any particular product. In numerous cases, American manufacturers will be able to compete in the Common Market, in spite of tariff discrimination, because of their strong technological lead and other advantages.

In its recent study of the balance of payments, the Brookings Institution[3] concluded that the loss in U.S. exports to the EEC of manufactured goods, because of tariff discrimination, would be in the order of 200 million dollars, on the basis of their projections to 1968.

On the basis of straight-line projections of the assumptions stated above as to rate of growth, and so forth, U.S. exports of manufactures to the EEC would increase from 1.6 billion dollars in 1961 to 2.3 billion in 1968. Allowing for the 200 million-dollar diversion of exports, estimated

[3] *Ibid.*

by the Brookings Institution, the estimate is reduced to 2.1 billion dollars. Because of the high degree of adaptability of a large proportion of American industry, this figure is probably an underestimate.

According to the U.S. Department of Agriculture, about 30 percent of all U.S. agricultural exports to the EEC comprise products that will feel the brunt of agricultural protectionism in the EEC, including feed grains, some wheat, and a few less important items, such as poultry. Among the 70 per cent of the products that will not be adversely affected by agricultural protectionism are such important exports as cotton and soybeans.

It would be incorrect to assume that the United States will be unable to sell any of the items included in the competitive list. The Brookings study concluded that the EEC's agricultural imports from the United States would be diminished by 350 million dollars below the level that would prevail, in 1968, if there were no agricultural import controls.

Without import controls, U.S. agricultural exports would increase, under the conditions assumed, from 1.2 billion dollars in 1961 to 1.7 billion in 1968. With the controls, the 1968 figure is reduced to 1.4 billion.

Non-agricultural raw materials include aluminum, copper, and coal. Because of the anticipated rapid growth of manufacturing in the EEC, it is not unreasonable to suppose that imports of these products will keep pace with the growth of the area's GNP. On this basis, imports of nonagricultural raw materials would increase from 673 million dollars in 1961 to 960 million in 1968.

Thus, under the assumptions stated, total imports into the EEC from the United States would increase to 4.5

billion dollars in 1968, which would still be an increase of 1.0 billion over imports in 1961. If the rate of growth of the gross national product of the EEC should decline to less than 5½ percent per annum, the estimated imports from the United States would show smaller increases. With a rate of growth of 4 per cent they would total 4.0 billion dollars, while, at a rate of 2½ percent (the recent rate of increase of the GNP of the United States), imports from the United States would be only slightly larger than in 1961. These computations are shown in Table 7.

Short-run Effects on the U. S. Balance of Trade

An increase in U.S. exports to the Common Market does not necessarily mean that the effect upon the U.S. balance

TABLE 7

Imports into the European Common Market
at Assumed Rates of Increase in
Gross National Product of the EEC

	1961 Actual	Projected to 1968 at Assumed Rate of Increase in GNP (in billions)			
		5½%	4.0%	3.0%	2.5%
GNP	$201.1	$292.4	$264.5	$248.0	$239.0
Total Imports	20.4	29.2	26.4	24.8	23.9
IMPORTS FROM U.S.	3.5	4.5	4.0	3.7	3.6
Manufactures	1.6	2.1	1.9	1.8	1.7
Agricultural	1.2	1.4	1.2	1.1	1.1
Raw Materials	0.7	1.0	0.9	0.8	0.8

of payments will be favorable in the sense that exports increase more than imports. As already noted, over relatively short periods of time imports tend to bear a rather fixed relationship to a country's gross national product. The gross national product of the United States is more than twice as large as that of the EEC. However, the ratio of imports to the U.S. gross national product is considerably smaller than is the ratio of imports into the EEC to that area's GNP. In recent years, imports into the United States have averaged only about 3 percent of GNP, compared with 10 percent in the case of the EEC. The share of U.S. imports supplied by the six Common Market countries has been averaging about 15 percent.

To estimate the effect of various rates of growth upon the balance of trade position of the United States, it is necessary to consider both exports and imports. Increases in the gross national product of the EEC will have the effect of stimulating U.S. exports to that area, while conversely, increased growth of the GNP of the United States will be accompanied by increased imports.

In Table 8 a comparison is given of projections of trade to 1968 at assumed rates of change in the gross national products of the United States and the EEC. Column 1 shows the actual magnitudes in 1961, while columns 2–6 project these figures on the basis of the stated assumptions as to rates of growth of the respective GNP's.

Column 2 projects exports and imports to 1968 on the basis of the rates of growth that actually prevailed during the period 1953–1961, in dollars of constant purchasing power. Under these assumptions, U.S. exports to the Common Market would increase to 4.5 billion dollars,

TABLE 8

Short-run Effects of the Common Market upon the
U. S. Balance of Trade, Projected to 1968
(in billions)

Projections to 1968 at Assumed Rates of Change in the
GNP's of the United States and the EEC

	1961 Actual (1)	(2) U.S. @ 2½% EEC @ 5½%	(3) U.S. @ 3% EEC @ 4%	(4) U.S. @ 4% EEC @ 4%	(5) U.S. @ 4.8% EEC @ 4.2%	(6) U.S. @ 5½% EEC @ 3 %
U. S. exports to EEC [potential]	$ 3.5	$ 4.5 [$ 5.0]	$ 4.0 [$ 4.5]	$ 4.0 [$ 4.5]	$ 4.1 [$ 4.6]	$ 3.7 [$ 4.2]
U. S. imports from EEC	2.2	2.8	2.9	3.1	3.2	3.4
Excess, exports over imports [potential]	1.3	1.7 [2.2]	1.1 [1.6]	0.9 [1.4]	0.9 [1.4]	0.3 [0.8]
GNP (EEC)	$201.0	$292.4	$264.5	$264.5	$268.2	$248.0
GNP (U. S.)	518.2	616.1	659.2	681.8	719.4	754.0

while imports into the U.S. from the Common Market countries would increase to 2.8 billion, yielding an excess of exports over imports of 1.7 billion dollars (compared with an excess of 1.3 billion in 1961). These figures take into account the anticipated diversion of U.S. exports of manufacturers and agricultural products by virtue of establishment of the common external tariff and the movement toward free trade among the EEC countries themselves. The figure in brackets (2.2 billion dollars) is the projection, leaving out of account these diversionary effects upon U.S. exports.

Some might maintain that 2½ percent is too low an estimate for the future rate of growth of the GNP of the United States, and that 5½ percent is too high for the EEC. In columns 3–6 the projections are made on different assumptions with respect to rates of growth of the two areas. Column 5 uses the rates suggested by the Council of Economic Advisers to the Brookings Institution in requesting the report that was published by Brookings in August 1963.

The columns, from left to right, show an increasing rate of growth for the United States and a decreasing rate of growth for the EEC. In the column at the extreme right the recent rates of growth of the United States and the EEC are practically reversed. It should be observed that, even under these assumptions, there would still be a favorable trade balance of 300 million dollars, even after allowing for the diversionary effects on U.S. exports of tariff discrimination by the Common Market. In terms of the over-all balance of trade effect, however, with the exception of column 2, all of the net changes would be smaller than the 1.3 billion-dollar excess of exports over imports in 1961.

It should be emphasized that these figures show only the differential effects on merchandise trade of various rates of growth in the GNP's of the United States and the EEC. No account is taken of capital movements, earnings on invested capital, or of military expenditures in Europe.

Long-run Effects of the Common Market on the U. S. Economy

In the long run, after the economies of the United States and Western Europe have had time to adjust, there should be flourishing trade between the United States and Europe, provided that the movement toward integration in Europe continues and that there is not a reversion to intensified protectionism on either side of the Atlantic. The very fact that the Treaty of Rome could be agreed to, with its provisions for free trade within the Common Market area and with its statement of willingness to negotiate with the outside world for eventual reductions in the common external tariff, is more important than the fact that there is a temporary reversion to nationalistic restrictionism under pressure from President de Gaulle. Also, the fact that Dr. Ludwig Erhard, a champion of liberal trade, has become Chancellor of West Germany is of considerable importance, as is the fact that there has been no letup in the enthusiasm for an outward-looking Europe on the part of such sponsors of integration as Jean Monnet, Walter Hallstein, and Robert Marjolin.

Historical experience and economic logic are more important, in the long run, than projections into the future of what appear, at any particular time, to be functional relationships between aggregates that happen to be statistically measurable. The concept of functional relationships between gross national products and relative price levels on the one hand, and merchandise trade on the other, sometimes does more to obscure long-run economic cause and effect relationships than to clarify them. At best, the concept of aggregate demand is vague and rather meaningless as far as economic causation is concerned. The determinants of imports, like the determinants of most other transactions, are individual price relationships, including prices of cost-items, as well as prices of products sold, in a vast sea of changing relationships. Changes in demand and supply conditions for individual commodities that are important in international trade are more important than aggregate relationships over an extended period of time.

History has demonstrated that industrialization and international trade stimulate each other. The experience of Great Britain and Germany at the turn of the twentieth century is a case in point. Both countries were industrializing, both were seeking markets for their manufactures, and trade in manufactures between them flourished.

Similarly, the external trade in manufactures of the United States increased as industrialization intensified. The most important single fact to keep in mind in judging the probable long-run effects of economic integration in Europe upon the United States is that, for the first time, there is to be a Europe—or at least, a large part of Europe—within which trade is to flow freely. Historically, the countries of Europe insulated themselves against competition from each other by erecting rigid customs barriers. By integrating their economies the European Economic Community is now forging a new economic entity, in many respects similar to the new entity that was created in 1787, when thirteen states comprising what is now the United States adopted a Constitution providing for the elimination of all tariff barriers among themselves and for the imposition of a common external tariff. There is good reason to believe that the establishment of free trade on the continent of Europe will give rise to tremendous economic growth. The gross national product of all of Western Europe, not just the EEC, is less than two-thirds as large as that of the United States.

The world is again witnessing a laboratory experiment, testing Adam Smith's famous dictum that the wealth of an economy depends upon the breadth of its markets. An area that, for centuries, has been divided into a large number of independent entities, separated from each other by restrictive trade barriers, is about to be consolidated into a new entity within which trade is to be unfettered. Specialization of production will be stimulated, markets will be broadened, and the wealth of the new entity will increase. It seems reasonable to expect that the growth of Western Europe will follow the pattern of the growth of the United States during the past three-quarters of a century.[4]

---

[4] Even a straight fifteen-year arithmetical projection of the figures shown above, on the basis of a 5½ percent per annum growth in the gross national product of the EEC, indicates an increase of over 24 billion dollars in the total external imports of the EEC. If the United States were to retain its present proportionate share of this trade, this would mean an increase of over 4 billion dollars in U. S. exports to the EEC.

American manufacturing industry is remarkably resilient. It must not be overlooked that our export industries are our strongest industries. They are the ones that are best able to take economic adjustment in their stride. American ingenuity, American styling, and continued emphasis on research and development should make it possible for American industry to compete with European producers in an expanding European market. The principle of comparative advantage is still operative, and it is almost certain that, in the reshuffling of specializations that is bound to occur, the United States will emerge with a long list of products that it will be able to sell competitively in Europe, in spite of discriminatory tariff walls. Of course, the adjustments will be easier to the extent that discrimination is eliminated and tariff walls lowered.

The impact of European integration upon U.S. exports of raw materials probably will be less than the impact upon manufactures or agricultural products, since most existing tariffs on raw materials are low, and the use of nontariff protection will be limited to a few commodities. The interest of manufacturers in securing cheap materials and fuel usually is overriding. A few commodities, such as vegetable oils, cork, flax, and hemp are produced in certain EEC countries and may be given favorable tariff treatment. Apart from these items, however, the principal Common Market tariffs on raw materials will be low. As Western Europe expands, its energy needs will increase markedly and there will be increasing need for fuels from the United States, including coal. In the long run this is not an unreasonable expectation, even though at the moment petroleum supplies in Africa and other parts of the world are increasing, and coal producers in Europe enjoy high protection.

Also, as the European economy expands, there will be increases in the demand for imported food, even though much of European agriculture is protected. Growth of the economy will call for increasing quantities of products now comprising approximately 70 percent of our present agricultural exports to the EEC, that are not competitive, including cotton and soybeans.

It seems reasonable to expect that, as the economy of Western Europe expands, as much as half of its total imports from the United States will not be seriously competitive with European production.

It may be significant that, within the past few years, since the beginning of tariff discrimination by the Common Market, U.S. exports to the Common Market have increased more than its exports to other countries. It may also be significant that, during the past few years, since both the EEC and EFTA have been reducing their internal tariffs ahead of schedule, U.S. exports to the Common Market countries have increased 5 per cent (between 1960 and 1962) whereas to the EFTA countries they have declined 14 percent. This would seem to indicate that the imposition of a common external tariff, thus far at least, has not been as restrictive of U.S. exports as the establishment of free trade among the respective members of the two regional groups, since the EFTA has no common external tariff. In any event, history seems to show that international trade accompanying substantial industrialization will flourish, in spite of tariff barriers.

In addition to the trade effects of the Common Market, there will be effects from capital investment in the EEC and the earnings from them. Formation of the EEC and the EFTA promptly induced American business firms to expand their manufacturing operations in Europe, so as to avoid tariff discrimination. Whereas in earlier years only about 15 percent of all new direct U.S. investment went to Western Europe, the proportion during the past few years has been closer to 40 percent. The bulk of the new direct investment of U.S. capital in Europe is in manufacturing enterprises. Capital outflow for this purpose increased from an annual average of 140 million dollars in the 1950–1955 period to nearly 450 million dollars in 1956–1960. To Europe, the increase has been from an average of less than 20 million dollars to over 200 million a year.

It is undeniable that, in the short run, the migration of capital to foreign countries diminishes the demand for American labor and aggravates the balance of payments problem of the United States. However, the long-run effects will be quite different. As Western European prosperity increases, and its total economy advances at a rapid pace, there should be increased demand for U.S. merchandise. Also, the larger the total American investment in Europe, the greater will be the aggregate return on investment. Again, if history can be a guide, we can expect that the U.S. balance of payments position within the next few decades will be greatly improved by virtue of recent and present new investment by Americans abroad. This was the experience of Great Britain during the nineteenth century. In the earlier part of the century huge quantities of British capital were invested abroad, particularly in North and South America, which had the effect of stimulating British exports. By the 1870s, however, earnings on existing foreign investment came to exceed the outflow of new capital and there was a net excess of receipts over outflow, making it possible for Great Britain to increase its merchandise imports and raise its level of living.

In the long run, a prosperous Europe is more advantageous, from the point of view of both American labor and the balance of international payments, than a stationary, or contracting, European economy. This has been the history of industrialization everywhere. As industrialization has advanced, there has nearly always been fear of increased competition, but the long-run effect usually has been larger per-capita incomes for everybody.

Conclusion

The Treaty of Rome creates a preferential tariff system that, in the short run, will divert certain U.S. products away from the European Community by discriminating against imports from nonmember countries. Certain U.S. exporters to the Common Market will encounter increasingly restrictive and discriminatory trade barriers. There is no automatic assurance that European regionalism will lead to greater cohesion of the Free World, since there is always a possibility that the new arrangement might become a bloc that will discriminate against outside trade and capital. Much depends upon the attitudes of the leaders of the countries involved. Regionalism based on expansionist concepts will lead to greater, rather than less, international prosperity.

It is important that the leading trading countries outside the new regional groupings exert their influence to ensure that the regional arrangements will be consistent with the expansionist principles set forth in the General Agreement on Tariffs and Trade. The most effective way for the United States to minimize the discriminations resulting from the common external tariff and the establishment of internal free trade in Europe is to reduce its own trade barriers drastically, on a reciprocal basis. The Trade Expansion Act of 1962 gives the President more power than ever before to do this, but it still does not go far enough in this direction. The only way to eliminate discrimination by a customs union, whether it be by the Common Market or by the British preferential tariff system, is to bargain tariffs and other trade barriers down to zero.

One of the most important features of the Trade Expansion Act of 1962 is that for the first time the law contains provisions making it possible for the President to invoke provisions to assist industries, firms, and individuals in adjusting to increased import competition through retraining programs, relocation allowances, and technical assistance to firms. For the first time in U.S. tariff history the law recognizes that the exclusion of competitive imports is not the only way to protect individuals against serious injury resulting from competitive imports. It is too early to know how this part of the statute will be administered, just as it is too early to know whether, in the forthcoming "Kennedy round" of tariff negotiations in Geneva the contracting parties will be disposed to move firmly in the direction of free trade. From a purely economic point of view, the greatest gains will be realized when trade is free and when countries can specialize in producing the goods that they can produce most effectively. The simple principle is that consumers will benefit when human and material resources are utilized to their maximum advantage.

DATE DUE